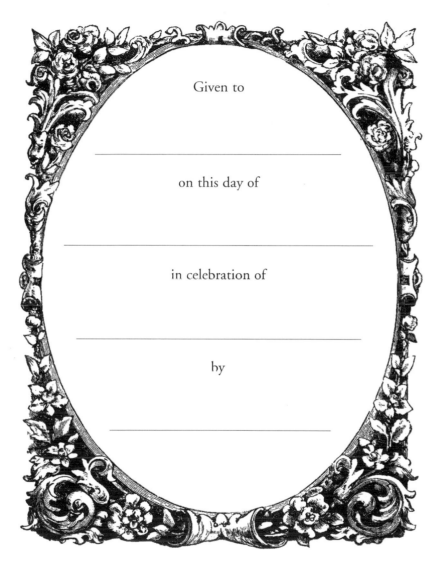

Given to

_____

on this day of

_____

in celebration of

_____

by

_____

A MOTHER'S LEGACY

Wisdom from Mothers to Daughters

COMPILED AND WRITTEN BY
BARBARA RAINEY
AND
ASHLEY RAINEY ESCUE

A JANET THOMA BOOK

THOMAS NELSON PUBLISHERS
Nashville

Published in Nashville, Tennessee, by Thomas Nelson, Inc.

Scripture quotations noted NKJV are from THE NEW KING JAMES VERSION. Copyright © 1979, 1980, 1982, 1990 Thomas Nelson, Inc., Publishers.

Scripture quotations noted NIV are from the HOLY BIBLE: NEW INTERNATIONAL VERSION®. Copyright © 1973, 1978, 1984 by International Bible Society. Used by permission of Zondervan Publishing House. All rights reserved.

Illustration on pages iii, 7, 47, and 95 by Mary Cassatt, *Mother and Child*. From a private collection, Paris, France/Giraudon, Paris/SuperStock.

Library of Congress Cataloging-in-Publication Data

Rainey, Barbara.
A mother's legacy: wisdom from mothers to daughters/compiled and written by Barbara Rainey and Ashley Rainey Escue.
    p. cm.
Includes bibliographical references.
ISBN 0-7852-7007-8 (hc)
1. Mothers. 2. Motherhood. 3. Motherhood—Religious aspects—Christianity. 4. Mothers and daughters. I. Escue, Ashley Rainey. II. Title.
HQ759 .R27 2000
306.874'3—dc21
                                                                    CIP
                                                                    99-085984

Printed in the United States of America
1 2 3 4 5 6 QPK 05 04 03 02 01 00

And so our mothers and grandmothers have, more often than not anonymously, handed on the creative spark, the seed of the flower they themselves never hoped to see—or like a sealed letter they could not plainly read.

—Alice Walker, *Wisdom Quotes*

To my daughters (and Ashley's sisters) who are not yet mothers—Rebecca, Deborah, and Laura—and to my granddaughters who are yet to be born. May you learn from those who have gone before you.

CONTENTS

PART THREE: A MOTHER'S LOVE

ACKNOWLEDGMENTS

We have enjoyed writing this book so much, but most of all we have been honored by the dear women who so willingly contributed to this book. Their stories have encouraged us, delighted us, and made us smile. We trust that you will feel the same as you read these words of gratitude and praise, honor and grace. Special thanks to each person who contributed not only your story, but also your valuable time. Thank you for graciously taking all our phone calls and providing pictures, names, and what must have seemed like a myriad of details. You have allowed us to see a fuller picture of God's love, grace, and mercy as you wrote about the tapestry of glory He is creating through your life experiences. Our hope and prayer is that many young mothers will be encouraged and will gain a greater vision for their irreplaceable role as mother.

I (Ashley) want to thank the Lord for allowing me to experience the gift of motherhood. I am just beginning to see the impact my life will have on my children's lives. I also want to thank my husband, Michael, for his support and love while I was writing. I've always dreamed of writing a book, and because of his encouragement, I was able to realize my dream. Together we are taking the brave step of faith to trust the Lord with our finances so I can be a full-time mom. I'm loving every minute of it!

I also want to thank my mom for the invaluable gift of being involved in my life and helping me grow in all areas of life. Thank you for helping me even now as I learn to be a mom. If I can do as well as you did, then I'll be doing great! I am so thankful that you chose to model sacrificial love every day as you cared for my siblings and me.

I (Barbara) am also grateful to God for the truly awesome privilege of being a mother. There is no other calling I'd rather have. Investing in my children has been my joy and my life's focus for more than twenty-five years. Nothing else I've accomplished even comes close to the importance of that investment.

My husband, Dennis, has lovingly pushed me to try all sorts of things I never would have done on my own. His vote of confidence made saying yes to this project that much easier. I am grateful to the Lord for my husband, my friend.

Together we both offer our thanks to Janet Thoma for asking us to write this book. The vision was hers initially. She was eager to give Ashley the opportunity to broaden the skills she'd learned in college as a journalism major and mentored her as they worked together. Janet is a real professional, and her years of experience provided novices like us the help we needed to successfully create a book.

Two other women, Dorothy English and Cherry Tolleson, helped us track down phone numbers, addresses, fax numbers, e-mails, and so forth so we could stay in touch with all the contributors as the project progressed.

Finally, we'd like to say that we wish we could have included many more stories. As I've talked to friends during the writing process, I'd think, *I wish we could have gotten her story.* So many mothers have given unselfishly to so many daughters. Writing this book was like searching for gemstones in a mine—every story of honor made us want to discover more. Perhaps that will be part of our journey in heaven, listening to the stories of how God used mothers to shape the destiny of the children He gave them. What a joy that will be!

Barbara Peterson Rainey
Daughter of Jean Peterson

—◄—

A MOTHER'S MODEL

The most important occupation on the earth for a woman is to be a real mother to her children. It does not have much glory in it; there is a lot of grit and grime. But there is no greater place of ministry, position, or power than that of a mother.

—Phil Whisenhunt

A mother is profoundly influential. For good or for bad, a mother marks her children. She gives us our first picture of what it means to be female. Her very presence shapes the way we feel and think. For nine months she literally enveloped our entire existence. One author states it this way: "The connection between a child and his biological mother appears to be primal, mystical, mysterious, and everlasting."[1]

Adam said of Eve in Genesis 2:23 (NKJV), "This is now bone of my bone, and flesh of my flesh." And so also are we daughters intrinsically connected to our mothers in an infinite number of ways.

Since time began, women have been born with a nesting instinct and have been nurturers. We are the builders and keepers of the home, the place where children *and* parents grow and mature—and individually become the people God intended them to be. When I was a new mom, one of the books I looked to for guidance and direction was Edith Schaeffer's *What Is a Family?* Twenty-five years ago I highlighted this passage that defined the home and the kind of atmosphere I wanted to create for my new little family:

> A home combines the shelter from physical storms and floods . . .
> with the reality of tiny growing or adult human beings finding the
> shelter they need from intellectual, emotional and spiritual attacks.

The family and home are meant to be the environment where human beings can find shelter, warmth, protection, and safety in each other. But for any four walls or flapping canvas or the jagged rock sides of a cliff home to really become "home," there needs to be a homemaker exercising some measure of skill, imagination, creativity, desire to fulfill needs and give pleasure to others in the family.[2]

This description makes me think of an incubator, an apparatus that creates and controls the ideal environment for a tiny baby chick or baby human to thrive and grow. Every day that a mother lives with her child, she is incubating him or her. Her life is the atmosphere that her child lives and breathes in.

My mothering years began with great expectations and high hopes. The nine months of pregnancy followed by the pain of childbirth is the process God designed to transform a woman

Barbara with Ashley at age two

into a mother. The joy I felt with each new baby was an incredible experience. But within weeks of the birth of my first child, Ashley, my many inadequacies and my first fears for the future confronted me.

Concerns about whether she was getting enough to eat, whether she was sleeping enough, or whether I would ever get enough sleep again occupied my thinking. Mothering was clearly a full-time job. I was suddenly aware of an acute need for all the help I could get.

Then my sweet, precious, innocent, fragile newborn turned into a toddler who ran away when I said "Come here," who avoided my eyes and continued to press on when I said "Don't do that." She began to throw her food off the high-chair tray and do all sorts of things I'd never dreamed of when I first held this tiny bundle in my arms. As a mom I began to feel frustrated; suddenly it seemed I was losing control. This little person actually had the potential to control me!

In spite of those frustrations, I loved and delighted in those early years, as we added a new baby about every two years. It was so much fun participating in their discovery of the world—watching them learn to walk, seeing them find a frog and toddle after it as it hopped away, taking long afternoon walks on Pine Valley Road with the littlest one in a stroller and two or three others walking or running beside me. Life was an adventure, and every discovery was a thrill.

The bigger battlefield of parenting for me, however, was the teenage years. Here's where a mom's own emotional maturity is challenged. This now thirteen-, fourteen-, fifteen-year-old daughter begins to express emotions of anger and fear—and they come out in ways the child does not understand. Because of the fluctuations in hormones, her emotions go haywire.

One day my teenage daughter was relating to me like an adult, the next day almost like a grade-school child again, and then another day as half-adult, half-child. Here's where I had to avoid entering into the emotional struggle on the child's level. *I* was the parent. She was the child. But that's easier said than done!

It has been difficult for me to always stay above the emotional fray, because I want so desperately to help my children, especially my girls, avoid many mistakes I made. I've wanted to convince them logically of the truth and for them to say, "Oh, I see, Mom. That makes sense. You are right." But they haven't been easily persuaded!

Many times I have been overwhelmed with the daily repetitiveness of my life, the endless needs of my six children and sometimes my husband, and the constant state of disorder in my home. Many times I have felt like a giant failure. Have you ever seen the T-shirt that says IF MAMA ISN'T HAPPY, AIN'T NOBODY HAPPY? That axiom reminded me that, as a mother, I set the tone in the home. The truth is, I was always in a position of influence with my children, but, I confess, I was not always interested in setting the tone. Many times I just wanted to pout or cry or complain or escape. I had no interest in being the adult and acting responsibly and maturely in front of my daughters and sons. It was in those moments, and there were hundreds of them, that I lost perspective. I forgot what the goal was, what the big picture looked like.

In retrospect, I wish I had taken more time off when life became overwhelming, like my friend Diana, a mother of five, who has a standing date with her good friend for every Monday night they can get away. Distance helps us see more clearly. But regardless of our circumstances or our feelings, I have learned that a mother's life is a significant model for the children that God gives her.

Now that I am on the finishing laps of my full-time mothering years, my daughter Ashley is just beginning her journey as a mother. I've already started the process of passing on to her some of what I've learned, just as I followed the example of my mother and she followed hers. Truth, wisdom, and practical advice were meant to be shared from one generation to another. That's what mothers do best. We teach as we go about life with our children.

But not all daughters have mothers they wish to emulate. Even if we all had admirable mothers, none of them was perfect. All moms have needed other models, mentors, and encouragers to help us when we didn't know what to do. And that is what this book is intended to do. Ashley and I want these stories to be practical illustrations in the textbook of mothering your mother handed to you. May the examples of these mothers fill in some of your blank pages, confirm the truths you already know, and add full color to your images of what a "good mother" looks like.

Come journey with us through this pictorial memory album of mothers. We have divided the book into three parts: "A Mother's Legacy," "A Mother's Lessons," and "A Mother's Love." Listen with your heart to the stories of a mother's influence on her daughter. Many mother-daughter teams have contributed, and it's interesting to see the similarities in what is passed from one generation to the next. Other mothers made deliberate changes as they transferred new or amended values and beliefs to their daughters. Some mothers were women of faith; others were not. These women lived and raised children on isolated farms, in small towns, in big cities, and overseas. Poor and wealthy, single and divorced, talented and intelligent, well-known and obscure, alcoholic and absent—all of these mothers profoundly influenced their daughters.

Perhaps you purchased this book for yourself. If so, the interactive pages will give you an opportunity to reflect on the stories as well as to note your own. If you purchased the book to give to a friend or a new mother, you can pass on your own thoughts about mothering by writing on these pages. This book is meant to celebrate motherhood.

What a surprise! In this day of broken families and burgeoning day care, mothers are often left feeling that they are dispensable, that the nurturing of children can be done by anyone. But as you may already know or will soon discover, *there is no substitute for a mother's love.* Mothering is a challenge and privilege. To know that your very existence will deeply influence your child is a strong motivation to make sure that your influence is what you want it to be. Jean Fleming says in her book *A Mother's Heart,* "It is remarkable that God allows us a part in shaping this child that He has created for His glory." May you find in these pages the encouragement and inspiration to mother your children with hope for their futures.

PART ONE

A Mother's Legacy

My mother and me when I was three

MODELING COMMITMENT

Nobody knows of the work it makes
To keep the home together,
Nobody knows the steps it takes,
Nobody knows—but Mother.
—Anonymous

*G*rowing up in the fifties was idyllic. World War II was over, and peace and prosperity pervaded much of American life. Neighborhoods were safe, friendly places where children played together, and stay-at-home moms visited over backyard fences as they hung their laundry on the line to dry. From my vantage point as a child, there was nothing to fear and everything to enjoy.

But were there things to fear? Yes. Was my peaceful childhood just the result of living in a time when the culture was family friendly? No.

Now that I am a mother, I can see and understand some of the fears and potentially damaging issues my mother lived with and successfully managed. I was born in a time when polio was the dread disease. Mothers everywhere must have feared for their children. But I was not afraid even when the little boy across the street who was one year older than I contracted the disease and became crippled for life. My mother never communicated a sense of panic or fear about what might happen, even though she must have felt it at times. She modeled a quiet serenity and trust.

My mother lived with great personal loss. Her only sibling, a brother just two years older, was shot down over Germany while on a bombing mission during World War II and was never found. A year after she married my father, her own parents decided to end their marriage. She has since told me of traveling to Arkansas from Chicago on the train with me as a baby in tow to spend a week begging and pleading and crying, all in an attempt to convince her mother to stay with her father.

Unsuccessful, she boarded a train in Little Rock for the long trip back to the Midwest, fourteen hundred miles from her now-separated parents, to continue the task of building her own marriage and family. With great distance and pain separating her from her own mother, it would have been nice for her to have had a warm, accepting relationship with her mother-in-law, who lived nearby. But that, too, never happened. She was never loved and accepted by my father's mother for reasons none of us ever knew.

Clearly, the "American dream" society I grew up in was *not* the reason for the peace and security I felt as a child. The source was my mother. Her nurturing and her faithful, uncomplaining presence created that atmosphere of safety in my life.

Author Elisabeth Elliot often quotes Psalm16:5: "Lord, you have assigned me my portion and my cup" (NIV). My mother modeled that verse for me in her quiet acceptance of the circumstances God ordered for her life. She had every reason to give in to despair and depression in those early years of her marriage. She could have sown the seeds of endless discord by ridiculing and rejecting one or both of her parents. She could have pitted them one against the other. She could have poisoned us as children against both sets of grandparents with angry tirades and outbursts about the hurt and rejection their failures had caused her. She could have criticized my father for the long, hard hours he worked and made him the scapegoat for his mother's attitude and difficult visits. She could have done all this and more, but she didn't. She never verbalized negative words about any of these important people in our lives. As a result, my brothers and I grew up confident of our parents' love for us, secure in their commitment to each other, and free to enjoy relationships with our grandparents.

From my mother's example I learned the supremely important lesson of not giving full expression to everything one thinks and feels. Her life exemplified the Serenity Prayer: "God, grant me the serenity to accept the things I cannot change, the courage to change those things I can, and the wisdom to know the difference."[3]

During my childhood and into my teen years, my mother did for me all the things her mother had done for her. She made almost all my clothes, and they were beautifully made. She faithfully cooked healthy, delicious meals three times a day, week after week. She made sure we all went to church every week, and she, too, was involved in church, teaching children and cooking for church and community events. She was a model housewife.

But more important to my brothers and me, and now to my own children, was and is her steadfast commitment to my father and their marriage. I haven't been able to discern whether this commitment was born out of a resolution she made on that train ride back to Chicago after seeing her mother end her marriage, or whether her love and devotion for my father was so strong that a lifelong commitment was obvious. Perhaps it was both. Whatever the reason, she has been faithfully committed to my father for over fifty-one years.

Mother left an indelible mark on me. She modeled commitment in marriage. I don't know what storms they weathered, but I do know my mother was willing to follow my father to the Chicago area to live in what must have seemed to her, a south Arkansas farm girl, a foreign land. She supported my dad when he went to night school to earn his master's degree. My father lived and worked in Pittsburgh, Pennsylvania, for a year and came home only on weekends. My mother faithfully kept our lives going during that time. After I'd left home, they packed up everything they owned, sold their house, and moved to Indonesia for a two-year consulting job. She could have said no many times along the way, but she didn't.

That commitment motivated me to write my parents a written and framed tribute as their Christmas gift in 1987. Though I originally wrote the following paragraph to both of my parents, it is no less true of just my mother. Making a marriage last a lifetime takes total commitment and devotion from both partners. As I wrote these words, I cried tears of love and gratitude for who they are and what they had given me.

> *The last gift I mention is in no way the least. In fact, it is probably the greatest because it is foundational to all the others: It is the example of your marriage. I cannot recall a single argument or disagreement between you. It was apparent that you loved each other, cared for each other, and liked each other. I never felt insecure or fearful that you would leave one another or get a divorce. I treasure that gift of your good, solid, happy marriage. I attribute a great deal of the success of my marriage to the example I saw in yours.*

I will be forever grateful for the far-reaching benefits of my mother's steadfast commitment to my dad and their marriage. Albert Schweitzer once said, "Example is not the main thing in influencing others; it is the only thing." My mother was a powerful model.

Barbara Rainey

↠———————↞

ONLY ONE MEMORY

The child you want to raise as an upright and honorable person requires a lot more of your time than your money.

—George Varky

If you could keep just one memory of you with your mom, what would it be? This is a tough question for most of us, since the time spent with our moms can hardly be narrowed into one event or memory. But if you could only keep one, what would it be?

For me it was a trip my mom and I took the summer before my senior year in college. I never had a high-school senior trip like many kids, so Mom and I decided we'd better take a trip while we had the chance. My mother loves antiques. She got me interested in them when I was little by helping me pick some dishes that I liked and then helping me look for them on our trips.

I began my collection of blue-and-white dishes for my future home when I was ten. Mom taught me how to save and plan for the future as she helped me find good buys. And my love for other antiques grew as we shopped together over the years. By the time I was sixteen, I was as interested in antiques as my mom, so for my senior trip we decided to travel by car to some small towns and shop along the way.

We set out on our five-day trip with a spending allowance from Dad and a bed-and-breakfast guide. We traveled from Arkansas into Tennessee, Kentucky, and Missouri, stopping anywhere that fit our fancy. We bought quilts, dishes, cameras, buttons, knickknacks, and gifts for family. We stayed in old homes (bed-and-breakfasts) all along the way.

One of the places where we stayed had a claw-foot bathtub.

That night we got in late, and we wanted to get an early start the next morning, so Mom suggested we leave right after breakfast. But after breakfast I told Mom I wanted to take a shower in that old tub, just to see what it was like. I remember her laughing and asking me afterward if it was better than a shower at home. Of course it wasn't any different, but I loved the experience. Now my husband, Michael, and I live in a house that is almost one hundred years old and we have a claw-foot tub, so I get the experience every day—it's wonderful! I really appreciate my mom not hurrying me off to accomplish our list for that day, but instead allowing me to enjoy something that probably wasn't very important to her.

The most important feature of this trip was the quality time with my mom. As one of six children, I did not have a lot of one-on-one time with each of my parents, so that time was invaluable. On my trip we talked about marriage (although I wasn't dating anyone at the time) and what was important in finding and choosing a mate. Mom gave me advice and thoughts on how to feel better about myself.

As we entered stores filled with old-fashioned sewing machines, handmade lace, Depression-era glass, old dressers, cabinets, and stained-glass windows, we explored a world that was passing away, and we found memorabilia we'd never seen before. I would pick up a dish or a bottle (I also collect old bottles) and tell her I liked it. If she didn't agree with me immediately, I began to question if I really wanted it or not. I'd hold on to the item as we walked around the store. I have a high need for verbal approval, and I tend to run from conflict or rejection.

Sometimes I would buy the dish, and sometimes I would change my

Mom and me
◄←

mind. Finally I realized that it wasn't that Mom didn't think the items I had chosen were good, it was that she considered her thoughts more before she responded. I saw that her opinion was well-thought-out, and it became more meaningful to me. Other times she really didn't agree with me, and that was good too. She forced me to make my own choices and stick with them. I was challenged to think on my own, and I tried to be more thoughtful about what I said or did.

On that trip I discovered in a new way how different I am from my mom and how well we complement each other. I'm likely to jump at a new idea or experience. "Hey, Mom," I'd say. "This might be fun. Let's do it!" Mom is more reserved and less impulsive. But often she will go along just to please me, and she ends up enjoying it as much as I do.

I am reminded of another experience we had on that trip. We were traveling over the Fourth of July weekend, and we decided to see the fireworks in one of the small towns we were in. We sat in a parking lot looking at some old buttons we had bought that day and waiting for it to get dark. Our trip was almost over, and we'd be meeting the rest of the family in Missouri in two days. We talked about our trip and just enjoyed each other's company. When it finally got dark, we got out to watch the fireworks. They were pretty good for the size of town we were in. When they were over, I remember being a little sad that we weren't with the rest of the family the way we usually were. When we met with my dad and brothers and sisters, we found out that our city had postponed its fireworks for three days due to dry weather. I was so excited that I would get to see fireworks twice that year. Mom and I laughed that at age twenty-two I was so excited to see fireworks twice. Fireworks aren't that big a deal to most people, but I loved it—fireworks on the Fourth and then again with my family. What a blast! I don't think Mom would ever have gone to two fireworks displays in one week without my urging, but I know she enjoyed them (probably because I did). Mom became more than a mom on that trip—she became my friend.

Our friendship has continued to deepen as I enter new phases of life, first as a wife, and now as a mother. On this trip I saw how much she provided balance for me and how wise my mom really is. This discovery has made me value her and her friendship more and more every day.

My mom made me feel valued because she took a week out of her life to spend it with me. Now as I look around my house I see bits of our trip here and there, and I am reminded of my mom and the finer things in life—relationships. Mom didn't go on that trip with me so she could buy some more antiques for her home or mine (we have plenty), but rather to invest in me. She has devoted her entire life to being my mom, and this trip was just another step in the journey of building a legacy in my life that would last when she is gone. This investment will continue to live as I pass on the value of relationships to my children and they to theirs.

Ashley Rainey Escue

➳─────────◄

Dottie McDowell
Daughter of Doris Youd

THE DELIGHT OF CHILDREN

Make a memory with your children;
Spend some time to show you care.
Toys and trinkets can't replace those
Precious moments that you share.
—Elaine Hardt

y mother told me the same thing over and over and over. I heard it from the time I was tiny until May of 1998 when she went home to be with the Lord. She always said it with enthusiasm, deep conviction, great warmth, and a twinkle in her eye. And I never got tired of hearing it. As a matter of fact, I have made a point of repeating the same message to my own children—again and again and again.

"Dorothy," my mother would say, "there is nothing more important or fulfilling than being a mom. It's the greatest and most challenging job a woman can have." My mom not only said it, but she also modeled it.

How did this make me feel? Secure and significant, because I knew that my mom was both happy and passionate about her job of raising my brother, my sister, and me. Frankly, I'm not at all sure how she learned her skills. Her own mother died of pneumonia when my mom was six months old. Although her father adored her, he was not able to care for her on a daily basis, so my mom found herself growing up in an endless string of summer camps, boarding schools, and foster homes. Perhaps these experiences made her long for the strong, stable mother-child bond that was missing in her own life, which caused her to be fiercely determined to provide it for her own children. I'll never know. But one unique and very powerful ingredient that I consistently observed and felt in her mothering was that *she delighted* in us—and consistently told us so.

How was this expressed to her children? She was always there for each of us. Mom not only wanted to be friends with us, but she also said how much she enjoyed us and how much fun we were! Very often, where other mothers would consider childish shenanigans as annoyances, inconveniences, or manifestations of rebellion, my mom would interpret them as acts of great creativity, expressions of potential, or sheer entertainment.

Consider these wise and merciful responses to three acts of mischief:

The first took place because, as a child, my hero was Peter Pan. When I was five years old, I sprinkled Ivory Snow (flakes of laundry detergent) through the entire basement, pretending I was Tinkerbell and spreading pixie dust everywhere. I vividly remember the feeling of exhilaration! When my mom discovered what I had done, she laughed. Instead of being angry, she took me on her lap, asked me to tell her the whole story of Peter Pan (once again), and lightheartedly helped me clean up the mess. This had a profound impact on my own parenting in years to come. You see, first she lovingly expressed that she delighted in me, and then later she tenderly and sensitively helped me to see the difference between acceptable and unacceptable behavior.

The second episode took place not long after that. When I was in kindergarten, I convinced my entire class to run away from school during naptime (when the teacher would predictably disappear into a back cubicle). My home was on the next street, and I challenged the children to explore outside with me when I gave the signal. I also made them promise not to stop for any reason. Each one eagerly agreed. With my heart pounding in anticipation, I gave the awaited signal, and we raced down the street together. By the time the teacher realized what had happened,

Dottie McDowell at age two with her mother, Doris Youd

twenty exuberant kids were halfway to my house.

When we arrived, there was great celebration—until the teacher appeared! My mom met her at the front door with warmth and a sense of humor, and then calmed the frazzled woman. Later I definitely got a lesson in appropriate versus inappropriate school behavior. But instead of being angry, my mother used this incident as an opportunity to applaud leadership qualities and to plug the benefits of discernment. You see, first she lovingly expressed that she delighted in me, and then later she tenderly and sensitively helped me to see the difference between acceptable and unacceptable behavior.

The third episode happened a few years later. My parents had carefully planted some peach and plum trees in our backyard, and it had taken several summers to finally have fruit on those trees. I immediately saw the fruit as an irresistible opportunity to make money! With boundless enthusiasm, I organized a backyard carnival and picked all the fruit to use as prizes. It was an enormous success! Of course, by the time the carnival was over, all the long-awaited peaches and plums were gone. Instead of getting angry, my mom praised my creativity, bragged about my entrepreneurial abilities, and said there would be other years for fruit.

Now, don't get the wrong impression and jump to the conclusion that I was never disciplined. Quite the contrary! My mom had an uncanny ability to discern whether my motives were motivated by childish fantasy or by deception and disobedience. And she responded accordingly. What I do know is that she was brilliant at using opportunities to convey to her children how much she delighted in them and how much she loved being a mom. As a child, I found this comforting. As an adult, it has motivated me to communicate the same message to my own children again and again and again.

REFLECTION: *How can you lovingly express your delight for your children? How can you tenderly and sensitively help them see the difference between acceptable and unacceptable behavior?*

Dottie McDowell is the mother of four children—one son and three daughters. She and her husband, Josh, live in Texas, where she helps him with various ministry projects. She has been a staff member of Campus Crusade for Christ for more than thirty years. Dottie has also coauthored several children's books with her husband.

Jeanne Hendricks
Daughter of Edna Robertson Wolfe

—◆—

A RESPECT THAT GREW

*Pampering a child is equivalent to teaching him that he is too weak
or incompetent to do things for himself. Therefore, he never develops
a sense of realistic accomplishment.*

—T. L. Brink

The mother God chose for me was a woman who could never
be described as "good ol' mom." In many ways Edna Wolfe did
not fit the often-portrayed image of a soft, maternal, all-compe-
tent, ever-available, albeit a bit worn around the edges, helping
hand. She was born to a Maryland farm family during the first
month of the twentieth century, grew to a prim five feet, three
inches, and never weighed much more than a hundred pounds.
Of Scottish descent, she approached life seriously—no nick-
names or word games from her. A woman of few words, I soon
learned that when she spoke, I had better listen.

In His all-knowing wisdom, God gave my mother a capable
and faithful husband who was warm and personable, with a
ready smile and an understanding word. I easily became
"Daddy's girl," but Mother's no-nonsense approach to life evoked
my deep respect. When I had chicken pox or boyfriend problems—or any other of a daughter's endless dilemmas—her advice
was always sensible and unruffled.

And her composure was always contagious. On one occasion
during my early teens, Mother was sick in bed, and I eagerly prepared a light meal with soup and crackers. In my haste I stumbled as I was going upstairs. The tray fell down the steps; the
soup splashed through the bannister and down onto the piano—
Mother's beloved piano! I came unglued! Still ringing in my ears

are her soothing words, "Honey, it's all right. You meant well, and I thank you for what you were doing. Now just go downstairs and get a damp cloth." Even now, decades later, I sometimes ask myself in mid-crisis, *What would Mother do?*

Although we lived in a large city, Mother communicated agrarian values. Her knowledge of and respect for plants and animals, her insistent appreciation for hard work, and her clear-eyed honesty formed the unspoken pillars of our home. Although her physical stamina was limited, her mental tenacity never wavered.

Mother never missed an educational opportunity. Whatever she had not been able to study in her younger years, she tackled later. Bible school, advanced tailoring, and banking occupied her adult education. A remarkably diverse library of books was part of her legacy to me. She had a working knowledge of auto mechan-

Jeanne Hendricks at seven months with her mother
————————————◂◂

ics, and was one of the first women in our neighborhood to qualify for a driver's license. During the Great Depression she "made do" with whatever was at hand. Since she excelled at handwork, she deftly altered used clothing without complaining and recycled leftover food. Mistakenly, I concluded that she lacked feeling and was indifferent and uncaring.

The day came when I said good-bye to her in a train station, ready to leave for my new world of an out-of-state college campus. As we parted I noticed a tear in her eye. I couldn't remember ever seeing her cry before then, and during that long train ride, I started to think about my mother much differently.

Midway into my freshman year, Dad called and asked me to come home right away. "Your mother is seriously ill," he said, "and I need you." For the first time in my life I began to see Mother—we never called her Mom—as one who needed me. She was so appreciative of everything I did. She got better and insisted that I return to finish the semester. Mother became my most vocal cheerleader because she was immensely proud that I was going to college, something no one else in our family had done.

Mother's most difficult trial began when Dad became terminally ill with inoperable cancer when he was in his mid-fifties. For ten long months Mother tended Dad as he lay in a hospital bed in their dining room. By the time he died, they had spent all their savings and had exhausted all their resources. Two weeks after the funeral, Mother called to tell each of her daughters, "I am entering the hospital for long-postponed surgery, and I fervently pray that God will not allow me to waken from the anesthesia." In her modest way she said good-bye.

Incredibly, she awoke to discover that a job application had been accepted; insurance benefits were activated; and all her hospital expenses were covered. Widowhood, after thirty-six years of marriage, was a daunting ordeal, but her courage taught all of us who knew her how to handle it gracefully.

Even though she was middle-aged, Mother went back to school and eventually became a bank teller, overseeing international transfers for a major downtown bank. Gingerly, she worked with a stockbroker to tuck away small slices of her salary. When she retired ten years later, she allowed her church to send her as a replacement field secretary to a mission station in the mountains of Mexico.

Just after returning home, an alumni group from her Bible school invited her to join them in a study trip to Israel, her lifetime dream. Because she had wisely invested her money years before, she was able to finance the trip, and it proved to be a highlight of her life.

Mother organized her tapes and pictures from the Holy Land trip and began to share them with women's groups in the rural area where she lived. Numerous women—women who had attended church all of their lives but had never heard the good news of God's grace—received Christ personally because Mother always accompanied her presentation with an evangelistic message.

Realist that she was, Mother voluntarily gave up her driver's license when she inadvertently ran into a stop sign, but she valiantly continued to live alone in her little house, even though her health was declining. During one particularly harsh East Coast winter, my husband and I invited her to visit us in Texas. We loved her lavishly and made her laugh, and her health improved dramatically in those memorable days. She read the Bible almost constantly and often discussed spiritual things, frequently mentioning that she wanted the Lord to take her home. He quietly and quickly answered her prayer; we feel honored to have shared her last days.

I do not remember Mother ever lecturing me. Shy, diffident, and reluctant to bring attention to herself, she nevertheless taught me by vigorously living the Christian life. Her lasting impact was to personify the axiom: My mother was not someone to lean on, but someone who made leaning unnecessary.

REFLECTION: *How did your mother show patience and model courage for you? What can you do to encourage these character traits in your daughter?*

Jeanne Hendricks is the mother of three adult children. Her firstborn, Barbara, died in January 1999. She also has six granddaughters. She is a teacher and author of several books, including *A Woman for All Seasons* and *Women of Honor.* She travels with her husband, Howard, who is chairman of the Center for Christian Leadership at Dallas Seminary.

Brenda Hunter, Ph.D.
Daughter of Maureen Hammond

— ✦ —

REDEEMING THE LEGACY OF LOSS

The family—that dear octopus from whose tentacles we never quite escape, nor, in our inmost hearts, ever quite wish to.

—Dodie Smith

One of my favorite children's books is *Love You Forever* by the Canadian writer Robert Munsch. It's the story of a mother who rocks her baby son nightly as she sings a simple song, "I'll Love You Forever."

The mother continues this nightly ritual across the years, through the son's messy toddlerhood, noisy puberty, rebellious adolescence, and—Munsch would have us believe—well into his adulthood. But one day, the mother calls her son to say he'd better come to see her because she is "sick and old." So later that night, the grown son steals into his mother's bedroom, picks her up, rocks her, and sings *their* song. Afterward, he returns home and rocks his baby daughter while singing "I'll Love You Forever."

As a psychologist, I find this book a beautifully simple statement about how love and emotional security are passed on from generation to generation. As a mother, I can recall similar touching moments with my two daughters. But as a daughter, I am aware that Munsch's book touches a deep, unfulfilled longing inside me for a mother-child relationship I never experienced.

My earliest memory of my mother is colored by sweet sorrow. I remember sitting beside her in an old swing on my grandparents' farm, listening as she sang "Swing Low, Sweet Chariot" in her soft, off-key voice. Widowed at twenty-two, Mother felt she did not have the emotional or financial resources to care for two daughters under the age of two. Therefore, she left me with my grandparents while she took baby Sandy to a nearby town to find work. On this particular summer day, her voice had a mournful quality that touched the deepest part of my being. Mother had lost her own mother to death as a young child, and I, for all intents and purposes, had lost mine.

Although I went to live with Mother when I was five, we were never emotionally close. Our emotional bond had been radically severed by a separation that was too early and lasted too long. Fortunately, I loved my grandparents dearly, and they loved me. Consistently warm and accepting, they provided a physical and psychological home for me until they died. I owe my humanity to them.

With my legacy of loss, it is not surprising that I had difficulty mothering my babies, or that I chose to put them in child care so I could teach at various colleges. Nor is it surprising that I skidded into a full-blown depression during my forties, when I finally confronted and reworked my relationship with my mother. Some would say that my passion—trying to strengthen the mother-child bond—grew out of my early pain.

Brenda Hunter at age four with her mother, Maureen Hammond

All of this is true. When I write or speak about the perilous cost of a child's early separation from her mother, I know of what I speak. I bear the scars. And though mine was an early and profound separation, when I worked on my doctorate in psychology at Georgetown University in my forties, I discovered decades of psychological research indicating that daily separations are hard for young children, and they leave a lasting mark.

Across the years Mother and I have had a difficult relationship, but recently something wonderful has happened. The Lord is working His alchemy, healing old wounds in Sandy, Mother, and me. Outwardly, Sandy and I are dutifully and generously caring for our fragile seventy-eight-year-old mother, who is in the latter stages of congestive heart failure. Inwardly, we are reworking the past and finding that as we nurture Mother, we mysteriously nurture the deepest part of ourselves.

The Lord has prepared me for this mother-daughter renaissance over the years as I have loved my daughters well and experienced

Brenda Hunter with daughters Holly (age seven) and Kristen (age five)

the committed, faithful love of my husband, Don. And for the past two years, I have joyously held and rocked my first grandchild, darling Austin, singing my own version of "I'll Love You Forever."

Long ago, Booker T. Washington said, "Success is to be measured not so much by the position that one has reached in life as by the obstacles which he has overcome while trying to succeed." I feel I've had enormous relational obstacles to overcome across the years. But today I am rich in friends and emotionally close to my immediate family. Moreover, I have put my legacy of loss to a useful purpose by encouraging mothers everywhere to be sensitive to the emotional needs of their young children. To surrender to the power of mother love. To sing a sweet love song to their children nightly. To love them forever!

REFLECTION: *Is there anything you need to seek to reconcile with your mother? Is there anything you need to ask God to heal?*

Dr. Brenda Hunter is the mother of two grown daughters, Holly Larson and Kristen Blair, and the proud grandmother of Austin Gregory Blair, to whom she dedicated her latest book, *The Power of Mother Love*. She is also a psychologist and internationally published author. Dr. Hunter has written numerous books for women, including *Home by Choice* and *In the Company of Women*. She and her daughter Holly coauthored *In the Company of Friends* while she and Kristen wrote *A Wedding Is a Family Affair*. Her daughter Kristen's essay is "Lessons in Integrity."

Transitioning from What I
Received to What I Will Give

As a mother, my job is to take care of the possible and let God take care of the impossible.

—Ruth Bell Graham

What things seem impossible ...
in what I inherited from my mother?

_____

_____

_____

_____

in what I want to give to my children?

_____

_____

_____

_____

Never forget:

You will never be a perfect mother.
God is the perfect parent,
And He still has trouble with His children.

A LEGACY OF TENACITY

The daughter is for the mother at once her double and another person.
—Simone de Beauvoir

*T*hat's it!" With those words my mother hung up the telephone, ending an exasperating conversation with her appointed caseworker. The call was her final push to get an answer to her request for government food stamps. Just a few years earlier she had been diagnosed with cancer and had managed without assistance. But now the frequent hospital visits for chemotherapy treatments had finally taken their toll on her body; her years of productive employment were now gone, yet her responsibilities as a mother and homeowner remained. Unable to work and declared disabled by her doctors, she needed help in order to feed herself, my adolescent brother, and me.

What was she to do but yield to what she believed to be indignation? She prided herself on being independent and self-reliant. Responsible. Committed. Hardworking. These words had characterized my mother. Now she felt beaten down and frustrated. Her current struggle to survive was a vivid reminder of how life had started to turn for her years earlier.

Mom was born in Philadelphia, Pennsylvania, one of the largest cities in the Northeast, a vast collection of humanity in all the sizes, colors, languages, and nationalities. She lived in a middle-class area with her mother, a custodial worker, and an adoring father, a well-known businessman and community leader. Grandpop was a proud man who shamelessly spoiled his three children, particularly the youngest, my mother. She could do no wrong.

Grandpop spent from ten to twelve hours a day, six days a

week, working in his business to provide for his family. The long hours away from his wife and family may have been a contributing factor to my grandparents' divorce, which was a painful experience for my mother. She adored her father and never really forgave her mother for "letting" him leave.

Some of my grandfather's drive rubbed off on my mother. She graduated from high school and enrolled in a local real-estate academy to pursue her desire to make money by selling property. During the day she worked in a deli shop and at night attended evening classes. The long hours, the mundane work, and the class load exhausted her. It was taking too long to achieve her dream, so she quit the academy. She was discouraged, felt alone, and got involved in a loveless relationship and became pregnant.

I was born to my unwed teenage mother just seventeen months after her high-school graduation. After I spent thirty days in the hospital's preemie incubator, Mom took me home to her mother's, where we would stay. The early days of planning and dreaming now were exchanged for long work hours and the exhaustion of motherhood. During the next two years she worked at the deli shop, trying to scrape out a living for us. I now had a baby brother as company. He would be "my" baby while mother was at work.

My grandmother, Nana, loved us but believed my mother would have been better off if she had married. At times, the tension between my mother and Nana made it impossible for them to remain in the same house. Therefore, we alternated between living with my aunt and my grandmother. Mom finally decided that life would be better for us if we lived in our own house. My grandfather's financial assistance and her meager savings gave us a start.

Cities are known for high-rise apartment buildings. Philadelphia had seemingly hundreds of thousands of people living in these twenty-story stacked apartments. Because of my mother's low income, she qualified to live in a government-assisted housing project. Our area of the city was called the concrete jungle. The projects were a haven for poor people like us, as well for teen gangs, alcoholics, and addicts. I remember the police-car chases, the screams of women being beaten by their men, the breaking of wine bottles in the stairwell, the stench of urine in our hallways.

Hopelessness and despair were all around us. Mom never allowed us to play outside on the playground because it was too dangerous with its rusty equipment and broken glass. She was very protective and planned to leave that neighborhood just as soon as she saved enough money to move us to a better place.

I was seven when Mom put me in charge of the household while she was at work. I was tall enough to cook at the stove, wash and iron our clothes, scrub and wax the floors, and care for my brother. He was my responsibility at home and at the nursery school. She drilled us: "Be safe, behave, be good, and do it right!"

Each day brought challenges to our small family. There was never enough money to pay all the bills, little tolerance for wasting food at mealtimes, and always plenty of secondhand clothing from the cousins. If we got a hole in our shoes, a matchbook cover was a quick fix! Mom gave us a castor oil-orange juice punch once a year to clean out lurking germs and give us a fresh start. We ate hot cereal every day, took daily cod-liver oil pills, and drank warm milk at night before bedtime so we would be ready for the cold winters.

The days were long and difficult for Mom: she worked each day at a deli and attended classes at night. Finally she completed her course work and received a certificate. Later this was her ticket out of the deli shop and into an established company as an administrative assistant.

We spent most Saturdays at Nana's. Mom understood that having a sense of family was important to her fatherless children, so we remained a close-knit family, even during those early turbulent days. Nana made each visit special. She cooked her famous meatloaf and Spanish-rice dish for dinners. She had the ability to make iced tea a sweet refresher; her lemonade required lots of lemons, which I gladly rolled and squeezed. Mom learned from Nana how to make big, round meatballs for her spaghetti. I will always be thankful to Nana for teaching Mom how to make cucumber salad. It is still one of my favorite dishes in summertime.

Mom taught me to enjoy cooking and how to be creative. I never remember her using a cookbook. She just knew what to do. After a great meal together, Nana, Mother, and my aunt and uncle would join other family members and sit for hours, just talking about neighborhood events and their many friends.

There were many informal moments of learning during our childhood. Mother saved her money and taught us how to manage ours. She often used Monopoly as a teaching tool. She would

Karen Loritts (bride)
with her mother,
Marlene Rodgers

set the board game on the dining room table and leave it out for days. She purchased all the big investment properties, like Park Place, and bought so many hotels and houses that when any of us landed on Park Place, we usually went bankrupt. Then Mom laughed with us at our disappointment at losing—again! She used that game to teach us to be patient, to make wise purchases, and to save some money for any coming financial bumps.

Years later, Mom used these same skills to purchase her first home. She researched and negotiated all the financing. Today that home is paid for. My younger brother is just like Mom when it comes to financial stewardship. He has never been in debt, waits to make large purchases until he can pay cash, and has seen his savings and investments work for his family.

Mom's tenacity, hard work, and endurance paid off. Once she was employed at a secure job, she was quickly rewarded with higher wages. She mastered the skills needed for the job and became invaluable to the company. She was very professional and competent. During my first year of college, I worked in the office she managed.

My mother learned many survival skills during her life as a single parent. I called her Miss Fix-it. She took care of leaks under the sink and relieved many a toilet of toys that had "accidentally" been flushed. She learned to sew so we could have a few new items, a real relief from wearing our cousins' hand-me-downs. She taught me how to sew and crochet, and I found these skills invaluable during my early years of marriage.

I could go on and on about my mom. She introduced me to the importance of home management and life skills that today have an impact on my own family. I have fond memories of spending many rainy and cold, snowy days inside with my own children, playing games, watching movies, reading, and even making applesauce for our breakfast biscuits. Mom taught me the importance of spending time with family.

Mom had tenacity—a real fighter's spirit—mostly because she had to fight to survive from day to day. Yet, late on the evening of September 23, 1989, her seventeen-year fight with cancer came to an end. Ironically, it was not the cancer that overtook her life; her heart just stopped beating during her sleep. The rest she really wanted and longed for had finally come. God had a sovereign plan for this woman, my mom, the scrapper—and she fulfilled it.

REFLECTION: *In what ways can you teach your children tenacity and financial stewardship?*

Karen Loritts is the mother of two sons and two daughters. She and her husband, Crawford, live in Atlanta, Georgia, where she is quite involved in her children's schools. Her oldest son, Bryan, has recently married, and Karen enjoys her new role as "mother-in-love" to her daughter-in-law, Korie. Karen is also on the leadership team for women's issues with Campus Crusade for Christ. She is the coauthor with her husband, Crawford, of *Leaving a Godly Legacy*. Karen serves on the FamilyLife Conference speaker team and actively participates in many local issues in her hometown.

Carolyn Wellons
Daughter of Frances Williams

—‹‹—

A PROVERBS 31 WOMAN

Mother love is the fuel that enables a normal human being to do the impossible.

—Author Unknown

any women spend years reading and rereading the well-known passage of Proverbs 31, the Bible's standard for a godly woman. I am one of the fortunate daughters who watched this passage being lived out by my mother every day of my childhood.

The passage describes a woman who "seeks wool and flax, and willingly works with her hands" (v. 13 NKJV). My mother is the consummate homemaker. She always made our home beautiful with her creative talents. Of course, I was unaware of her feminine genius until years after I had left home. Didn't everyone's mother make pleated draperies, sew slipcovers for the sofa, improvise patterns to her own liking, and even design tailor-made garments? I felt like a princess in her handmade dresses, satin and net formal gowns, and wool coats with matching satin lining and fur muffs.

Mother was the creator of all the costumes I wore for music recitals and childhood operettas. I loved wearing the yellow butterfly costume with sequined wings in the second grade. Up in my attic today is the glittering organza cape I donned as the fairy queen in the third-grade production. Years later, my daughter proudly wore it as the angel who proclaimed the birth of Jesus to the shepherds, when our family reenacted the Christmas story each year during the holidays. Soon my grandchildren will enjoy the magic of that beautiful translucent cape. Mother not only sewed for my sister and me, but she was also Dorcas to our extended family—altering and mending and giving of her talents to many.

Proverbs 31 also describes a woman who "rises while it is yet night, and provides food for her household, and a portion for her maidservants" (v. 15). Though I never was able to match Mother's expertise in sewing, I have followed her example of hospitality. Mother taught me the joy of beautiful table settings—replete with fresh flowers, sterling silver, fine china, sparkling crystal, beautiful linens, glowing candles, and delicious home-cooked meals. We always had the visiting preachers in our home for dinner. I loved our green Jell-O salad squares with a peach half strategically placed in the center and surrounded with chopped pecans.

Even the ordinary days at home were full of good food and freshly picked flowers from Mother's garden. My father came home from work for lunch every day, and we children walked home from school to eat a full meal, which always included homegrown vegetables, hot cornbread, and iced tea with plenty of sugar. Fridays were Mother's beauty shop mornings. On those days we knew there would be a big pot of spaghetti, made early that morning in case Hollis, the beautician, was running behind with her appointments. Mother showed me that providing delicious and healthful meals was an important part of her contribution to her family.

The Proverbs 31 woman also "watches over the ways of her household, and does not eat the bread of idleness" (v. 27). I volunteered my mother for every possible need in my life—and in the lives of most of my friends! She was always a homeroom mother—you know, the ones who planned and baked for every holiday party and drove for every field trip. Most of those growing-up years Mother served as president of the city's garden club, which included organizing a junior garden club for us children. I was proud of her magic with fresh flowers. I was her protégée and even once won a blue ribbon for a creative floral arrangement we made in a little cradle that we designed with white Popsicle sticks.

Mother hosted a Bible study in our home for my friends and me and had us memorize Scripture each week. While many other moms were too busy with other interests, she always was available and eager to be involved in her children's worlds. When I was in high school, she spent a week of each summer at cheerleading camp as our sponsor. I never thought about her sacrifice of time or comfort as she bunked in the hot dorms. At home, throughout the summers, she could be found in the early mornings picking vegetables in the garden my father grew in our backyard, then shelling and shucking and blanching and freezing the abundant produce.

The years passed too quickly for her, and soon she found her busy home much quieter as the children grew up. Then I saw her struggle to fulfill the vision of a Proverbs 31 woman whose "strength and honor are her clothing," who "shall rejoice in time to come" (v. 25). Just as she and my father were beginning to enjoy more time for each other, my father began running a

Carolyn Wellons with her mother, Frances Williams

chronic, low-grade fever. His diagnosis of lung cancer filled our hearts with sorrow. Following his death, Mother became extremely depressed; her aloneness was something she had not anticipated, and she felt forsaken by God. Slowly, she began to heal as she responded to the Lord's tender mercy and love. Mother's heart had been dealt a blow, but the Spirit within gradually strengthened her. I watched an incredible metamorphosis.

Mother had always been very industrious, capable, and able to accomplish a lot by her own indomitable strength. Now a new woman emerged—one who had been to Gethsemane alone and had encountered the living God there, one who had learned that no fear in life overpowers the love of Christ. Jesus became her all-consuming passion. Whereas she had studied the Bible for information and knowledge, now the Word of God became her life.

Mother began teaching a Sunday school class in her church and has continued doing that for the past twenty years. Several young women whom she has mentored have lived with her for a few weeks or a few months as the need dictated. For the last years of her parents' lives, Mother moved them into an apartment behind her home and lovingly cared for them until their deaths.

Mother became a bold evangelist, earnestly desiring everyone to experience the freedom she had found in Christ. She has boarded temporary youth pastors, high-school teachers, and other needy people for whom she has witnessed and prayed and cooked and blessed in the apartment vacated by her parents. My mother, the Proverbs 31 woman, extended "her hand to the poor" and stretched "out her hands to the needy" (v. 20). She opens "her mouth with wisdom, and on her tongue is the law of kindness" (v. 26).

I am grateful for the years I lived under Mother's tutelage, learning the beauty of homemaking and childrearing. But I have been even more blessed as I watched her transform a lonely life into one rich with the ministry of love and service. She fears the

Lord and loves and serves Him with all her strength, even as she approaches her eightieth birthday. Her works do praise her for her years of faithful living, but I proudly rise up and bless her saying, "Thank you, Mother—you truly excel them all!"

REFLECTION: *What was the difference between this mother's early years and her later years? Do you think one time period had more eternal significance than another did? What matters most in a mother's life, in the way she lives her life?*

Carolyn Wellons is the mother of three: Bill, Sarah Wood, and Ben. The latest excitement in her life is the arrival of her first grandchild, Fred Andrew Wood III. She lives in Little Rock, Arkansas, where her husband is a pastor. Carolyn is an active leader in various prayer groups at her church. She also enjoys mentoring younger women. She and her husband, Bill, have written a workbook for couples: *Getting Away to Get It Together.* Her daughter's essay, "Passages," follows this essay.

Sarah Wellons Wood with her mother, Carolyn Wellons

Sarah Wellons Wood
Daughter of Carolyn Wellons

—+—

PASSAGES

Spare the rod and spoil the child—that is true. But, beside the rod,
keep an apple to give him when he has done well.

—Martin Luther

*M*y mother celebrates her womanhood with a godliness that touches everyone around her. All of my life I have watched her seek the Lord. Many times I have entered a room to find her on her knees in prayer, or with her head bowed over her Bible. She has taught me by example to fear the Lord. But she did not leave it up to me to "catch" her example. Using her wisdom and creativity, she designed a series of celebrations for each passage of my life. We call these celebrations the "Godly Woman Legacy Ceremonies."

The first passage of my life was my thirteenth birthday. My parents took me out to dinner at a nice restaurant. They celebrated my entering a very important stage of life, the one in which I would become a young woman. Mom presented me that night with a challenge to remain sexually pure until marriage. She and Dad asked me to make this covenant with God—not with them—and reassured me of their constant support. I remember my mom telling me, "The rewards of your wedding night will be invaluable if you remain a virgin until then." She affirmed her belief in my wise decisions and godly discernment. I accepted this challenge, and Mom presented me with a gold key charm—a "purity key"—that I wore around my neck as a reminder of my covenant with God.

On April 18, 1998, the night of my wedding, I gave this key to my husband and, with tears, explained its special meaning in my life. Then I gave my beloved the most precious gift I had to give—my purity. The reward for me and for him that night was indeed great as we consummated our marriage.

The second passage of my life was my high-school graduation at age seventeen. Two of my aunts (Ann Parkinson and Sherard Lewis) and my mom—all pastors' wives—took me out to dinner. After each one shared the milestones she had observed in my life, they all took turns exhorting me to maintain a godly focus when I went to college. Mom encouraged me to live my life passionately committed to God and to be bold enough to say no to the bad influences around me. She stressed that I didn't need to conform to the world to be accepted, and that I was a leader in my own way. She encouraged me to have the confidence to maintain high standards. Doing so would be attractive on any college campus, she said.

Mom presented me with a gold botonée cross, which she had designed specifically to celebrate this passage of life. The date of my high-school graduation was engraved on the back of the cross, along with the initials of the three families who had joined to pray for me. The initials *W, L,* and *P* (Wellons, Lewis, and Parkinson) also stood for Wisdom, Love, and Purity. Mom asked me to wear the gold chain as a reminder of my commitment to the Lord and as a symbol of the virtues I was trying to keep.

Little did I know that college would give me the opportunity to make my faith my own for the very first time. I'm sure my mother knew this, and she prayed for me every step of the way. After my freshman year, I discovered that resisting the lures of our culture was difficult. I began to analyze what I believed and why, using a pattern my mother had taught me: to envision the future (to imagine how I wanted to see myself upon college graduation) and to consider what it would take for me to get there.

Soon I knew that my vision of the person I wanted to be would require committing myself entirely to God's will, which meant making some serious and difficult decisions. During the fall semester of my sophomore year, I asked my dad to baptize me to commemorate this recommitment. At the service, I wore the cross necklace my mom and aunts had given me upon going off to college. Now I felt its significance more than ever.

The third passage of life was my college graduation and marriage, and what a joyous one this was! During my junior year of college, I became engaged and was anxious to get home, where my fiancé waited. For this celebration, my mom, Aunt Ann, and Aunt Sherard took me out for a special dinner to commend my college achievements: my commitment to purity, and the many decisions I had struggled to make through the years. Mom presented me with the same gold cross she'd given me four years earlier, this time with a small diamond in the center to signify my worth as a child of God. After dinner when we were alone, Mom read a special letter she had written for this occasion. She honored my teachable heart, saying she believed it to be one of my greatest strengths. She affirmed my tender spirit for the Lord's calling in my life, and she envisioned great success for my future as a God-fearing wife. She breathed life into me with these words of blessing.

Learning to be a godly woman in today's culture is difficult, almost impossible, without a mentor and moral cheerleader. For me, that person has been my mother.

In celebrating the passages of my life, she gave me the legacy of godly womanhood. My mom passed her wisdom on to me— and what a blessing this is for me! I treasure that living legacy, and hope one day to pass it on to a daughter of my own.

REFLECTION: *Are there passages that you would like to celebrate with your daughter? Are there special ways you can mark them?*

Sarah Wellons Wood is the new mother of a son, Fred Andrew Wood III. Sarah graduated from Wheaton College with a degree in literature. She enjoys reading and writes and edits for *Excel* magazine, a publication in Little Rock, Arkansas. Sarah also sells children's clothes (Kelley's Kids) out of her home and does some tutoring while taking care of Andrew. She and her husband, Fred, live in Little Rock.

PART TWO

A MOTHER'S LESSONS

The Rainey girls having fun with finger paint

"WHEN I'M A MOTHER, I'LL . . ."

I begin to love this little creature, and to anticipate her birth as a fresh twist to a knot which I do not wish to untie.

—Mary Wollstonecraft

ave you ever said to yourself, "Someday when I'm a mother I'll *never* let my children do that" or "I *will* teach *my* child to . . ." If you are honest, the answer will be yes. All young women of marriageable age make those observations, judgments, and resolutions *before they have children.* Some of those pre-children resolutions are unrealistic, like one of mine: I promised myself I'd never let my children be seen in public with dirty faces and runny noses! Once I had children I realized this was a situation over which I did not always have control, and I soon learned to settle for a lot less.

Other determinations we make for ourselves as mothers are not so trivial. My mother made one of those promises to herself when she was a girl. Growing up on a South Arkansas farm in the thirties, she remembered coming home from school on a number of occasions to find her mother not at home, with no indication of where she had gone or when she'd be back. Her dad was out in the fields and not within reach.

She told me, "I remember being afraid that my mother wouldn't come back, so I decided that I'd never be gone when my children came home from school." It was an important resolution and one she kept. In all of my growing-up years, my mother was waiting for us at home. Or on those rare days when she'd gone to town and thought she might be late, she always left a note saying where she was and when she expected to be back. I never wondered where she might be or if she'd come back. Fear of abandonment was foreign to me because her personal experience had compelled her to make a significant change in her own mothering. My brothers and I were the beneficiaries.

As a college student in the late sixties, I was invited to a Bible study where I discovered what it meant to have a personal relationship with Jesus Christ. My parents had faithfully taken our family to church every Sunday of my life. I had been active in Sunday school and youth group as a teen. Yet somehow I had never heard that to become a Christian, one must invite Christ into his or her heart and surrender control to Him. For me this idea was revolutionary.

I became a part of what has been defined in retrospect as the Jesus movement. Just as the hippies and flower children of the sixties rebelled against the establishment, so those of us who discovered Jesus wanted to change much about the Church as we knew it. Formality and tradition had not served us well; it needed to be reformed. We were young, idealistic, and certain that we could change not only the Church but also the world. We also were sure Jesus would return before many of us got married and had children. But I remember thinking, *If He doesn't come back before I have a family, I want my children to grow up in a different kind of Church, knowing what it means to believe and how to become a Christian from an early age.*

Out of those life-changing experiences of my college years, I

Family dinner madness

determined to move from the more private faith of my parents' generation to the more expressive faith of my generation. This conviction influenced the spiritual direction of my mothering.

When my firstborn, Ashley, was still a nursing baby, I remember coming to a point of decision regarding my growing faith and the promises I'd made to myself about letting my children see my relationship with Christ on a daily basis. The details of the situation are not clear in my memory, but I'll never forget the choice I faced. For some reason I was angry with my new daughter. Perhaps she was crying because of teething, or maybe it was the first time she'd bit me and, because I was hurt, I felt anger toward her. Or it could have been that I was just tired from all the sleep deprivation new mothers feel.

Whatever the reason, I was angry, and I knew I was responsible for my emotions. Ashley had done nothing wrong. There was no intentional disobedience. She was just a baby. I remember thinking to myself, *It's no big deal. Just blow it off. So what?* But then I thought, *It all starts here. Begin now to do what's right.*

So I picked up my daughter, looked her in the face, and said, "Mommy got really angry with you, and I was wrong. Will you forgive me?"

I knew she couldn't answer me, but I knew she could sense my heart and know that I was at peace with her again. More than that, I knew that the next time it would be a little easier to apologize to her.

I've done a lot of apologizing over the years to Ashley and her five siblings. There were days when it felt that was all I did. And I'm still asking them for forgiveness.

One day when Ashley was five, she wanted to know what it meant to be a Christian and how to get to heaven. I was putting her to bed at night, and I'm sure I was tired. (I was always tired it seemed, even long before bedtime.) Her brothers were already in their bunk beds in the other room, and, because she was the oldest, she was last to be tucked in. Dennis had just kissed her and left her room. She still had me there, and she wanted to talk. Why is it that children always seem to ask these important questions at night when their parents are nearly brain-dead?

This was the moment I had imagined in college: the opportunity to lead my child to Jesus. But not quite how I'd pictured it. There had been no hints from her that day to let me know I needed to prepare for this bedtime question of eternal importance. For a moment I pondered my options. *Postpone it for another day when I'm more awake or go for it now in spite of my fatigue?*

In an instant I decided to explain what she needed to understand and do to receive Christ so she could be sure of going to heaven someday. Thirty minutes later, she said she understood and wanted to pray. I led her in a prayer, and she prayed after me. After she said amen, I hugged and kissed her and stood up to leave her room and turn out the light.

In two steps I was in her doorway, ready to leave, when I heard her voice coming from the now-darkened room. "Mommy," she said, "guess what? I saw pink elephants when I closed my eyes to pray."

Suddenly the feeling of pride and confidence that this long-anticipated moment had just produced drained from me like the air escaping from a punctured balloon. In that moment, all my idealistic convictions seemed hollow. Was that conversation a waste of time, a ploy by my daughter to stay up past her bedtime? Could I really expect to teach my children spiritual truths, or did they have to learn them later from someone else?

In those early days of mothering, my idealism and my dreams collided with reality many, many times. My notions of clean, well-behaved, curious children who wanted to have intelligent conversations with their mother about spiritual matters were too lofty.

Even though my expectations were often unattainable, my decision to teach my children spiritual truths was still reasonable.

I just needed the Lord to show me that it doesn't happen all at once, but in innumerable small pieces.

Deuteronomy 6:5–7 talks about conversing with your children about God's law, His truth as you go about daily life. It says, "These commandments that I give you today are to be upon your hearts. Impress them on your children. Talk about them when you sit at home and when you walk [or drive] along the road, when you lie down and when you get up" (NIV).

I have had a lot of "talk time" with my kids since I first became a mother more than twenty-five years ago, but our conversations haven't been just about their relationship with the Lord. There have been countless hours of instruction, teaching, and correcting on everything from setting the table correctly to telling the truth to obeying the rules on borrowing. Ruth Bell Graham has said, "A true mother is not merely a provider, housekeeper, comforter, or companion. A true mother is primarily and essentially a trainer."[4]

All the teaching about God's Word and how to live in this world shapes the boys and girls of today. They will become the men and women of tomorrow who will live responsible lives of purpose and dignity before the Lord who made them, and with the people God puts in their lives.

The six Rainey kids, blindfolded for a Family Night lesson

MOM, THE TEACHER OF LIFE'S MOST IMPORTANT LESSONS

The mother's heart is the child's school-room.

—Henry Ward Beecher

*D*o you think of yourself as a teacher? Many of you received an education in some field or profession other than teaching, just as I received my degree in journalism. Yet each of us is a teacher, maybe not to a class of students but to our children. The dictionary defines *teaching* as "imparting knowledge or skill," "instructing in," "causing to learn by example or experience."

Teaching makes up much of what we as moms do every day. With every word we speak and every action we take, we are imparting truths to our children. The lessons I learned from my mom have now taken on new meaning. I am looking down the road of motherhood and remembering the creative ways Mom invested in my life.

Mom loved to help us learn. She homeschooled me (and my brothers) until the sixth grade. She was able to give us good quality teaching time, which was particularly helpful when she and my father found out that I had a learning disability. They were told that I would probably never attend college (something I didn't learn until recently).

I struggled in school and had a hard time learning without extra help from my mom. I can remember the day when my parents told me that I might have to work harder than other kids do, but that I could make it if I really wanted to. My mom believed in me and took advantage of summer months to help my siblings and me learn new skills.

I remember how she helped us learn our states and capitals as we filled in maps on long car trips. She instilled in us a love for reading by setting up a reward system that paid each of us a penny per page for every book we read during the summer. Each summer we also wrote at least two or three times a week about our activities in notebooks she made for us called "vacation books." At the time we felt like we were in school, having to write and spell, but she was teaching us the importance of writing and journaling. Now my brothers and I enjoy getting out our "vacation books" and reliving those summer memories. Mom helped me make my books more creative and fun by encouraging me to pick flowers and, with help, to press them in my vacation books. She also took pictures for us to paste in our books to help us remember special events and trips.

Not all our lessons were related to academics. Mom taught me how to sew one summer, and I made some pajamas and a small pillow. She took the time to help me learn to cross-stitch and to sew a nine-patch quilt that now hangs in my home. She also taught me other domestic skills like cooking and cleaning.

Ashley and her mom pick flowers for Ashley's vacation book.

We had chores that we had to do every Saturday by noon. If we didn't get them done, we received extra chores. We usually had the same chores for a year, and then they would be rotated and we would be given new, harder chores. Through these chores I learned that being part of a family means pitching in and helping out around the house.

We also had nights when we were responsible for cooking. I learned how to cook from scratch and be creative with what was available. Everyone had a night when he or she was responsible for cleaning the kitchen. Sunday nights were a group effort that taught us teamwork and relational skills, because we had to communicate and work together to get the kitchen clean enough to pass Dad's inspection.

In today's culture of constant noise and rushing to and fro, Mom taught me the importance of having some quiet time daily with little or no activity. Each day when we were home, we had to spend an hour or two alone. We could read a book, take a nap, play quietly, or just sit and think, but we had to spend it alone and we had to be quiet.

Now that I am grown, I realize how important it is to have those times without intense activity. These quiet, alone times are havens in my days, whether I spend them reading a book or being with the Lord. I know that on many of those days when we were in our separate rooms alone, Mom was taking a nap or spending time with God. With six children our lives were very busy and, I'm sure, very demanding for her. Now I really appreciate the importance of spending time with no entertainment and without others around to distract me.

"Be still, and know that I am God" (Psalm 46:10) is one of my favorite Bible verses. How can we hear from the Lord if we are always busy and surrounded by noise? Mom took an active approach in helping me learn that I need to make time to be quiet and listen to the Lord.

My mom taught us by leading in these areas, and by being proactive in helping us grow in all areas of our lives. Now I am looking forward to passing on the lessons my mom taught me to my children as well as teaching new lessons along the way. My parents never encouraged us as children and teenagers to blend in with the crowd, but instead to stand up for what was right, regardless of the price. The result has been confidence in our faith and beliefs so that we can stand on our own now that we are adults. This is definitely a principle I want to pass on to my children as they grow.

Ashley wearing the nightgown her mom helped her sew

LESSONS IN INTEGRITY

*Parenthood is a partnership with God. You are not molding iron nor
chiseling marble; you are working with the Creator of the universe in
shaping human character and determining destiny.*

—Ruth Vaughn

$\mathcal{M}$y mother is a natural teacher. Not only is she the
oldest child in her family (a role that makes her
eminently qualified to tell others what to do), but she spent several years early in her career teaching the intricacies of English
grammar and literature to high school and college students. She
wholeheartedly embraced her role as mother and educator of two
little girls and became our guide in all matters moral, intellectual,
and emotional. Since I was a headstrong, lively child, I was
exposed to many lessons in integrity.

One day, when I was a five-year-old sprite with wispy hair, my
best friend, Cathy, and I were canvassing the neighborhood on
our bikes, looking for something to do. As we circled the block,
we noticed some lovely white rocks in a neighbor's flower bed. We
quickly loaded most of them into my white wicker bicycle basket,
which was festooned with pink plastic flowers, and pedaled furi-
ously back to my house. Once there, we proceeded to landscape
charming stone arrangements among my mother's pansies.

About a week later, while Mom was outside gardening, she
observed an abundance of rocks in her garden. When she asked
me if I knew where they had come from, I sheepishly confessed
to pilfering them from our neighbor. At this point, some children
would have been sent to their rooms or denied a slice of choco-
late cake at dinner. Not me. My mother took my hand and
together we collected all the rocks to return to my neighbor's

yard. Even now, twenty-five years later, I can remember how terrified and anxious I felt as I trudged down the street beside my mother. As I stood knocking at our neighbor's door, my legs shook wildly and my pulse raced. Fortunately, the neighbor was shopping, and my mother allowed me to return the rocks neatly to the flower bed. My mother later admitted to being amused by the whole experience, but to me, this had been a grave ordeal.

My experience with petty thievery left an indelible impression on my young mind. However, my conscience was still in its nascent stage. Soon after my rock garden escapade, our family moved to Asheville, North Carolina, and I entered Mrs. Newton's second-grade class at Asheville Christian Academy. I excelled academically and was fiercely proud of my spelling achievements. For several weeks running, I had aced all spelling tests, and I was committed to maintaining my unblemished streak. But as I sat taking my test one fall afternoon, I could not remember how to spell one word. So I furtively looked at the paper of the girl sitting next to me to verify its spelling, and then I turned my paper in.

That night, as I sat with my family eating dinner, I was racked with guilt. After the dishes had been washed, I could stand it no more. "I've done something bad, and I don't know what to do," I blurted out to my mother. As she listened to my agitated confession, she comforted me and suggested a solution. "Why don't we call Mrs. Newton," she said, "and ask her what she thinks you should do?"

Needless to say, that was *not* what I had in mind, but I glumly agreed (what else could I do?) and my mom dialed Mrs. Newton's number. She chatted briefly with my teacher, telling her that I had something I wanted to say. With my heart pounding in my ears, I grasped the receiver and explained that I had cheated on one of the words from that afternoon's spelling test and was very sorry.

Fortunately, Mrs. Newton was a merciful woman. After a brief conversation about the importance of doing my own work, Mrs. Newton thanked me for calling, saying she would only penalize me by marking down the fateful word. She then told my mother, "Lots of children cheat. But Kristen is the only one who has ever called to confess." I went to bed that night much relieved, confident of my clear conscience.

These early lessons about the consequences of stealing and cheating have been etched deeply in my mind for many years. Even now, I can vividly recall the intense emotions I felt. On those and other occasions, my mother taught me valuable lessons about the power of integrity. I did not realize then how fortunate I was to have a mother who loved me enough to gently and calmly allow me to face the consequences of my actions.

Now a mother myself, I know I will have many opportunities to teach my child the value of integrity. Several days ago, my toddler, Austin, was outside playing happily with some of the neighborhood children. As I looked up from a conversation with a friend, I could see him bent intently over a neighbor's flower bed. His chubby legs wobbled as he leaned forward to pluck one of her prized pansies. Amused, I hurried to rescue her flower from his determined grasp. As I lifted his wiggly little body to tell him her flowers were off limits, I laughed to myself. Truly, my life had come full circle.

Kristen Blair has worked as a writer and researcher on family issues for Empower America and for the federal government. She is the coauthor of *A Wedding Is a Family Affair.* Kristen lives in North Carolina with her husband, Greg, and son, Austin. Her mother's essay is "Redeeming the Legacy of Loss."

—◄+—

THE BEST SHE COULD

Happy children do not ask why their mothers or anybody else loves them; they merely accept it as a fact of existence. It is those who have received less than their early due of love who are surprised that anyone should be fond of them, and who seek an explanation for the love that more fortunate children take for granted.

—Anthony Storr, psychoanalyst

'm probably the least likely person to ever head a mothering organization like MOPS International (Mothers of Preschoolers). I grew up in a broken home; my parents were divorced when I was five. My alcoholic mother raised my older sister, younger brother, and me.

While my mother meant well—truly she did—most of my memories are of *my* mothering her, rather than her mothering me. Alcohol altered her love into something that wasn't love. I remember her weaving down the hall of our ranch home in Houston, Texas, a glass of scotch in hand. She would wake me at 2:00 A.M., just to make sure I was asleep, and then I would wake her at 7:00 to try to get her off to work.

Sure, there were good times like Christmas and birthdays when she went all out and celebrated us as children. But the nights always ended with the warped glow of alcohol, and what she did right was again lost in what she did wrong.

Ten years ago, when the call came to consider leading MOPS International, the vital ministry of nurture for mothers, I went straight to my knees—and then to the therapist's office. How could God use me, someone who had never been mothered, to nurture other mothers? The answer came as I gazed into the eyes of mothers around me and saw their needs mirroring my own. In those moments God seemed to take my deficits and make them my offering.

Not long after my mother's death in 1991, my brother compiled some of her writings into a bound book and presented a copy to each of her children. I was just finishing my book *Mom to Mom,* in which I traced my journey of motherhood from a sense of inadequacy to quiet confidence. I turned a page in my manuscript and then set it aside to pick up the book of my mother's words, and Paige Lee, my mother, dead and gone, leaped across the void of time and touched my life.

Finally I could see that she loved as well as she could. Her drunkenness obscured her love, however, and it took God's love to use my mother's alcoholism to shape my life.

I am who I am today because of my mother. From her I learned that creativity is my friend, and that if I think long and hard enough, I can think my way out of any difficulty. I gleaned a love for celebration and surprise through Christmases, birthdays, and friends. I discovered a love for reading and the blissful escape of journeying to other worlds through words when times were so

Elisa Morgan (center) with her daughter, Eva, and mother, Paige Lee

tough at home. God used her illness to shape my resilience. He used her withdrawal to carve me into a tenacious pursuer. He used her neediness to mirror my own. I became a survivor.

These are the positive lessons gained from the upside-down reality of living with an alcoholic. I am grateful for them, because they have been used to carve out character in my personality where there might have been deficits. A mother's love may sometimes fail, but God's love can take even the imperfect love of an imperfect mother and use it to shape His perfect design in the life of her child.

Thank you, Paige. I know now that you did the best you could.

This article first appeared in the May/June 1999 issue of *Christian Parenting Today* magazine.

REFLECTION: *Remember that God uses even our failures and mistakes and weaknesses in the lives of our children when they seek Him.*

Elisa Morgan is the mother of two, Eva and Ethan. She is also the president of MOPS International (Mothers of Preschoolers), an organization dedicated to meeting the needs of mothers of children from infancy through kindergarten. Elisa hosts *MomSense,* a syndicated daily radio ministry to moms. She is the author of several books: *What Every Mom Needs, What Every Child Needs, Mom to Mom, Meditations for Mothers, When Husband and Wife Become Mom and Dad,* and *The Mom's Devotional Bible.* Elisa lives in Aurora, Colorado, with her husband, Evan.

Vonette Bright at age two with her mother

HER LOVE SOMETIMES SAID NO

Morality, like art, consists in drawing the line somewhere.

—G. K. Chesterton

Mother believed in taking advantage of teachable moments, and those moments happened most frequently as I worked with her. Washing and drying dishes, preparing meals, cleaning house—these were Mother's communication times. Subjects were discussed, family history shared, ideas worked through, funny stories told, and lots of just plain fun was had. Through conversation Mother had a unique way to get people to share thoughts and to talk freely about any concerns. Somehow I never grasped her secret. Now I wish I had been more attentive to her technique.

Mother married at age seventeen, and I was born the next year. She grew up with her children and was totally devoted to us. Dad was fifteen years older than Mother. He was wise, understanding, and a good provider, but he left much of the communication with the children to her. We loved Dad and knew he loved us, but we confided in Mother.

When I was about thirteen, she and I began to talk about boys. As I now think about it, these conversations were probably the result of the "kissing club," the brainchild of some girls in my seventh-grade class. "Could the club meet at my house after school?" they asked one day.

I knew why they suggested my home. We had a laundry room attached to our garage where the guys could wait to be blindfolded and then brought outside one by one to be kissed by the girl who had chosen them—the girl's way of telling the guy she liked him. Never mind that neither I, nor probably most of the half-dozen other girls, had ever been kissed. This was probably true of the guys, too.

Mother was not home when we arrived, and I knew I was not supposed to take friends into the house when she was not there. But there had been no instruction about the garage—and only the guys would be there. Everything else was out in the open. It did not occur to us that our parents would object. I certainly had not thought about what my mother would think; she was always happy for my siblings and me to have friends over to play in the yard after school.

About the time the second or third girl had given her kiss to the guy (on the mouth with eyes wide open), Mother appeared on the scene. Fortunately I had not had my turn. Instantly she put an end to the club's first—and last—meeting. In a small town word spreads fast, and I'm not sure that Mother didn't rush home from afternoon marketing because she already had word that our kissing club was meeting in her backyard. Ever since that time I have had to live with the family "disgrace," which has now turned to laughter.

Obviously, I needed a bit of instruction on boy-girl relationships, and from that day on, Mother looked for every opportunity to do so. She began by explaining that kissing must be held in reserve for a person you have come to know very well—likely the person you will marry. There are only so many ways to show physical love, she said, and we need to be very careful with whom we display affection. Mother made it clear that I should never kiss a guy on a first date and that I should be very cautious about even holding hands until I had been acquainted with a guy for some time.

One evening a young man in my high school, who tried to get a good-night kiss after a date with me, said, "I hope you will not compromise your standard. The guys are making bets as to who will be able to break your resistance." That made for quite a few dates and for lots of fun, but no kisses.

I can laugh about the innocence of the kissing club now, yet I learned a supreme lesson in discernment and the importance of not going along with the crowd. Today sex has become so recreational that some seventh graders easily find themselves pregnant with no more thought of the consequences and implications than I had of a casual kiss on the lips.

How grateful I am that Mother loved me enough to say no many times. She took the time to develop a relationship where I learned I could trust her judgment and confide in her freely. It paid off. There are no skeletons in my closet, and that contributes greatly to a happy and lasting relationship in marriage.

REFLECTION: *What moral standards will you encourage your children to take? Are you willing to stand with your children, so that they will not be alone when they are taking a stand for the truth?*

Vonette Zachary Bright is cofounder of Campus Crusade for Christ, along with her husband, Dr. William R. Bright, which they began in 1951. Even with all her achievements, Vonette says that her favorite titles are wife of Bill, mother of Zac and Brad (their two grown sons), and grandmother of Rebecca, Christopher, Hamilton Keller, and Noel Victoria. She is the author of *For Such a Time As This* and coauthor of *The Joy of Hospitality* and *Building a Home in a Pull-Apart World*.

Joya Fortson with her mother, Toni, and sister, Sheila

Joya Fortson
Daughter of Toni Britt Fortson

—+—

VIRTUE AND FEMININITY

Mothers who are confident, proud of their own femininity, and nei-
ther jealous of nor in rebellion against their husband's masculinity
will be able to do a much better job in helping both their boys and
their girls to be comfortable and secure in their own sexual identity.
—Ruth Tiffany Barnhouse

Could it be that the agony of repeated, unasked-for advice, rules, warnings, discipline, laughter, tears, admonishing through Scripture, and even nagging, are all fragments of my mother's virtue that built and are still building her legacy in me?

Femininity has been defined as "a gentle, tender quality found in a woman's appearance, manner, and nature."[5] I am *not* by nature gentle. Nor am I tender. Yet my mother found ways of teaching my spirit this high calling. She started in the high court of God with examples from His leading ladies. With the wisdom God gives to mothers of impossible daughters (of whom I am, regretfully, chief), she wove the bold, intelligent leadership of the conquering Deborah in the book of Judges and the efficient, independent, wise businesswoman of Proverbs 31 with the submissive keeper of the home, the modestly adorned, graciously spirited example in 1 Peter 3. She did it in the disguise of everyday life. Had I known that she was trying to make a lady out of me, I would have revolted. My mother led my sister and me to embrace femininity through the following virtues:

She taught us the *virtue of submission* by teaching us to yield our rights. Often Mother required us to yield the right to wear pants and instead don a dress if the eyes of young men would be better served by our countenance. I, more than my sister, was admonished to yield the right of my opinion when the self-esteem of a male peer might be jeopardized (even if my idea was superior in every way!).

My sister and I learned the *virtue of hospitality* by watching our mother's face as she prepared to share her home and heart with whomever God sent to us. Mother was a firm believer in serving our guests with our very best, rejecting my ideas that paper plates and plasticware were just as noble as her china. Often I would remind her in vain that it is the heart, not the china, that counts. However, her joy of welcoming guests to our home endured even when the guests were gone and the dishes began to call from the kitchen sink. Her model has been wonderful to watch, and I look forward to making hospitality a priority in my own home someday.

Mother's confidence in God and His sovereignty instilled the *virtue of self-confidence* in us. "He makes no mistakes," she always said. And no mistakes included our being African American. My mother's dignity and the dignity with which she taught us our heritage convinced us that we were African American for a unique purpose. "Diversity is valuable and must be honored," she said. She taught us to be gracious to less-than-gracious people.

Mama drilled into us the *virtue of gratitude* by requiring us to write thank-you notes for every act of kindness anyone bestowed upon us. My sister and I also learned to appreciate a gentleman's graciousness in opening a door or carrying a heavy object. (This was so painful for me, since I felt no need for this service!) My mother frequently honored my father for his provisions and hard work in caring for our family, and she taught us to do likewise. She made gratitude the eleventh commandment.

Most dynamic, though never spoken, were her *lessons on being a lady*. "All females grow up to be women," she said, "but very few become ladies." In the African-American culture particularly, a generation of strong women has arisen, ungraced by the charms of gentle womanhood, unbalanced by the divine protection of femininity.

My mother wanted her daughters to understand that the women whose lives speak the loudest are often the women who are the quietest. She wanted us to realize that the best-educated women are those who know God's laws. She taught us that the most successful women are those who obey His Word, and she let us know that the strongest women are those who are not afraid to recognize their weaknesses.

We never had a specific lesson on femininity or on being a lady. The teachers of true femininity are always godly women—like my mom. One of her greatest legacies may be that her example caused me to desire to be a lady of God's kingdom in every way.

REFLECTION: *Am I teaching my daughter the virtues of femininity? Am I balancing my desire for her to be strong and independent with a desire for her to be a gracious lady?*

Joya Fortson is a biology major at Covenant College in Lookout Mountain, Georgia. In her spare time, she teaches piano and violin and writes short stories and articles. Joya is studying to be a doctor and would like to use her medical skills in the mission field after her training is completed. Her mother's essay in this book is "Serving As Jesus Did."

Lessons from a Mother to a Daughter

Mothers pass on their wisdom to their daughters, who pass on that wisdom to their daughters . . .

My mother taught me this lesson:

_____

_____

in this way:

_____

_____

_____

I want to teach my children this lesson:

_____

_____

in this way:

_____

_____

_____

_____

My mother was the most beautiful woman I ever saw. All I am I owe to my mother. I attribute all my success in life to the moral, intellectual, and physical education I received from her.
                    —George Washington (1732–1799)

Anna Dean Stephens Campbell
Daughter of Willie Fair Stephens

—•—

MY MOTHER ALWAYS SAID

Though Mom didn't give us a high standard of living, she gave us a high standard of life. It didn't matter how many rooms our little migrant house had. What mattered was what went on in those rooms.
—Linda Weber, *Mom, You're Incredible*

As my mind wanders back more than sixty years, I see my mother using a straw broom to tidy up the house. I see Mother's always-beautiful smile and her patience with all seven of us children. Daddy will be home soon, and then the family will gather at the dining room table for our evening meal. The ritual at mealtime: Waste not, want not. I see the family giving thanks to God with Daddy. This is a time each day we always enjoy, being together and listening as Daddy and Mother share their activities of the day, and we children share ours also.

I recall a number of maxims my mother used, like "Take what you have and make what you need." On one occasion during the Christmas season, Mother was in the kitchen. She had just baked a cake. While the layers were cooling, she started getting the frosting ready. She cooked the mixture too long, however. Rather than throw away the whole batch, she buttered a platter and poured the hot concoction in it. Later she broke it up for us children to eat as candy and made another batch of frosting for the cake. Mother taught me how to take what I have and make what I need! How often through the years I've found myself following her example with my own ten children.

Willie Fair Stephens, Anna Dean's mother

By her example Mother taught me the

73

art of loving and nurturing children and family. So often through the years I've had a bed full of children. When they were small, our ten always knew they were welcome to cuddle with Mama! I adapted that from my mother's tenderness to me and my siblings. And the legacy goes on as our grandchildren feel free to always give hugs to Grammy and receive in kind.

I'm often reminded of our Sunday morning rituals. After breakfast Mother would get all seven of us ready for Sunday school and morning worship. Once Sunday school was dismissed, we all knew to take seats on our family bench. We also knew that God's house was sacred, and we were to be on our best behavior. A look from Mother, without her usual smile, and someone was in trouble!

On April 6, 1938, Mother was called from our earthly family. Of course, her passing left a huge void! I'm always thankful in my heart for God's blessings to me and my siblings for such a caring and devoted mother—and the legacy goes on.

Anna Dean Stephens Campbell is the mother of ten children, thirty-eight grandchildren, and two great-grandchildren. After trying for seven years to have children, she was told she would never be able to have any. She and her husband, Emanuel, adopted a girl while living in Japan. After that she gave birth to nine children. Anna has always wanted to write and has written for some church publications. She also was quite active in her local school district and worked there after all her children were grown. Anna Dean and her husband live in Kansas City, Missouri. They have just celebrated their fifty-first wedding anniversary. Her daughter's essay, "Lessons in the Kitchen," is next.

Robyn Campbell McKelvy

Daughter of Anna Dean Stephens Campbell

⊸⊱⊶

LESSONS IN THE KITCHEN

Cooking is like love.
It should be entered into with abandon or not at all.

—Harriet Van Horne

I remember thinking that I must be dreaming when I smelled the sweet aroma of bacon as it wafted its way to the third floor that Friday evening. It was 5:00 P.M. and, just like so many times in the past, the smells from the kitchen of our old house called me from wherever I was to our central gathering room.

As I entered the kitchen, I saw each of my five sisters going about her specific tasks. Immediately I was given a job. "Make the orange juice, Robyn," Mom said. As I got out the pitchers and the frozen juice, I thought about the joy that was in that room as we Campbell girls prepared the dinner meal for our clan of twelve. Laughter was always in that room. Later that evening, as we all sat around the table for our dinner, there was so much excitement. We had never had pancakes with all the trimmings for dinner before.

Now I am the mom and I have learned a few lessons, subtly taught by my mom's example.

> Year after year, meal after meal, with no complaints,
> she set food on the table for us to eat together.
> *I learned endurance.*
> Everything was always the temperature each item
> was supposed to be (no microwaves then).
> *I learned timing.*

75

The table was always set with food in the center,
forks and napkins to the left of the plates.
I learned presentation.
We always had room for one more
no matter who the person was or where he or she came from.
I learned hospitality.
Everyone pitched in and was gently instructed by Mom.
I learned delegation.
We never wondered if there would be a meal.
There always was,
at the usual time, three times a day.
I learned management.
At times we children complained as we saw
dishes like stewed tomatoes or lima beans on the table.
I learned the importance of balance and gratefulness.
Each of us learned to do whatever job we had with all our might.
Selfishness was never an option or attitude.
We all learned to serve.
The laughter in the kitchen
carried over many times to the dining room table.
I learned to have fun.

The prayers in the kitchen as she prepared our meals equipped each of us future moms. The conversations from simple to serious, the one-on-one instruction, the training . . . and finally, pancakes and trimmings for dinner with no one knowing that was all we had.

I learned creativity.

Mom taught me (and continues to teach me) a lot of life's lessons, but one very important one—I love to cook!

Robyn Campbell McKelvy is the mother of seven children: Raychel, Ray Jr., Ross, Ryan, ReNay, Raegan, and Ravin. Robyn attended the University of Missouri, Columbia and Calvary Bible College, where she studied music. Robyn is a full-time homemaker and enjoys spending time with her children, playing the piano, and sewing. She and her husband, Ray, are members of the FamilyLife speaker team. They live in Kansas City, Missouri, where Ray is a pastor. Her mother's essay is "My Mother Always Said."

Jean King Peterson
Daughter of Zelma Everett King

LIFE LESSONS FROM THE FARM

Getting children to do their chores is an uphill battle for most mothers because they prefer being peacemakers and don't like to bicker. Conflict makes them feel inadequate. They assume other families have more responsible children who always follow through with their duties. This is a fantasy.

—Jean Lush

I was born on November 14, 1925, on a farm in south Arkansas. We lived in a two-room dogtrot farmhouse with a lean-to kitchen on the back. Our house was already more than forty years old when I arrived.

I had a brother two years older than me, a daddy who worked hard on the farm, and an old grandpa who lived with us. But from the beginning I knew my mother, and I knew that she loved me.

I don't know who was there when I was born, but I know who *wasn't* there. My mother's mama was not there to help her give birth to my brother or to me. Early in life I learned that my Grandmother Emma was not alive. Though no one talked about it often, certainly not outside the family, as a child I learned the sad story of my grandmother's death.

My mother was the oldest of five children. She and her family lived on a farm just a couple of miles from where I was born. Like most men in our rural area, her daddy was a farmer. My mother began attending school when she was seven or eight years old. Her brother soon joined her, followed a few years later by two of her sisters.

In October 1921, my mother, her mother, and sisters were in the kitchen making lunches for her brother and sisters who were still in school. As they were working around the table, standing side by side, they could hear their three-year-old sister, the delight of the family, playing happily between the kitchen and the next room. No one knows exactly what happened next or how it happened. Somehow the little sister found her father's hunting rifle and somehow fired it. The bullet hit my grandmother. She fell to the floor and died.

What grief my mother and her siblings must have felt! What guilt and endless self-accusations my grandfather must have faced! I'm sure that everyone wondered why such a tragedy happened, and they never got a satisfactory answer to that question. But life went on—as it always does.

My eighteen-year-old mother became the "mother" of the family. As the eldest child, she assumed all the responsibilities. Whether it was intentional or just intuitive, the family began almost immediately to protect baby sister from the unbearable knowledge that she had, though innocently, killed her own mother. They closely guarded that secret all their lives, for her best interest and her peace.

Soon after her mother's death, my mother married a boy on the neighboring farm who had just returned from World War I. As soon as they were married, she moved into his boyhood home and began to do what she'd been taught to do in her own home—keep house. Though she loved my father, their marriage was not the comfort or relief she must have hoped for. She had moved into *his* house, not *their* house. And actually it was not even her husband's house, but her new father-in-law's house. I'm sure Mother must have felt like a guest—or even a servant girl—cooking and cleaning for a father-in-law and an unmarried sister-in-law who weren't kind and welcoming to her. But she tolerated the situation because she knew, or at least hoped, it wouldn't last forever. Her sister-in-law eventually married and moved away, but her father-in-law lived to be one hundred years old. He died the year I was married. She lived in his shadow for more than twenty years.

I knew that Mother was unhappy much of the time, but as mothers often do, she focused on my brother and me—she delighted in us and loved us. Mother lived for our success and for our futures. She designed her own patterns and sewed all my clothes—from everyday dresses to dresses for church, graduation, parties, and even my wedding. She taught us everything and paid for others to teach us skills she couldn't teach.

When I was twelve, Mother and Dad took me to a hospital in Louisiana for a new, somewhat experimental, surgery to correct one of my legs, which had quit growing. She had researched and

Jean King Peterson
on wash day
at the farm

found that "cure" because she didn't want me to be handicapped in any way. Two years later, when I was fourteen and my brother was sixteen, she entered a writing contest and won an all-expense-paid trip to the New York World's Fair for our whole family for a week. Our picture was in newspapers across the state, and for the first time in our lives, all of us had brand-new, store-bought clothes!

But we learned the enduring lessons of life daily on the farm. I grew up learning how to work, because we were expected to work alongside our parents. I learned to cook, do laundry, feed the chickens, pick cotton, and garden. Mother always had a big vegetable garden, which supplied much of our food, but she

Zelma Everett King,
Jean's mother
——————◄◄

always found time and places for flowers in her gardens. Because of the hours we worked together outside, I learned to love gardening and developed a green thumb of my own, especially for growing all kinds of flowers.

Mother taught me to "do what you're told, the best you can." I don't remember complaining much, because she always worked with me. She gave me responsibility and praised me when I did a job well.

When I was fourteen, Mother had a summer job away from home. She gave me the responsibility of cooking our noon meal, the main meal of the day. I felt very grown up and was quite proud of my accomplishments, especially when my daddy and brother and grandfather complimented me.

Mother always helped with my homework and insisted that I study hard. She desperately wanted for my brother and me to go to college, something she always wished she could have done. Very few young people from our little town ever went to college, but Mother worked hard and sacrificed to see that my brother and I did.

We went to church and Sunday school every week. Our church was a little country Methodist church that couldn't afford to have a full-time minister. We had a traveling pastor who came once a month to preach to our congregation, and everyone in the congregation pitched in. My mother helped by teaching Sunday school and by working with our youth group when my brother and I were teenagers.

When I was old enough to date, Mother didn't give me many specific rules, but she did say, "I trust you to do what's right." All my life I had been a cooperative, obedient child. I had always wanted to please her, and that did not change when I began dating. Somehow Mother's trust in me worked. I always felt that if I did something wrong, she would know and that would shatter her trust in me. I couldn't do that.

Although I don't remember her actually saying the words *I love you* very often, I don't recall feeling deprived. I knew from all she did and said that she loved me unconditionally—that there was nothing I could do that would take away her love.

One of Mother's most unselfish acts of love was when I told her I wanted to marry a boy from Chicago. She knew that I would be moving nine hundred miles away, but she never said anything to influence me or to control my decision. This was just after my brother, her only other child, had been killed in the war. Mother put my happiness above her own. I married right out of college and moved north with my new husband, leaving her and my father alone on the farm.

My dear mother died twelve years ago. I still miss her, but I am grateful for all she taught me about life, love of family, and, most of all, love of God.

 **Jean King Peterson** is the mother of one daughter, Barbara Rainey, and three sons, John, Tom, and Jim. She has fifteen grandchildren and one great-grandson. She and her husband, Bob, like to spend their time traveling and visiting family. Jean's hobbies include sewing, which she does for all her grandkids, and gardening. She is always bringing new plants to Barbara for her expanding garden. Jean and Bob live in Camden, Arkansas.

Susan Alexander Yates with her daughter, Allison Gaskins

Susan Alexander Yates

Daughter of Frances Alexander

—<•—

THE STOLEN RUBBER BANDS

Good parents are not afraid to be momentarily disliked by children during the act of enforcing rules.

—Jean Laird

*W*hen I was growing up, it never occurred to me that Mother was anything special. Instead, at times I was sure that she was the meanest mom in town. We weren't allowed to watch TV on school nights, and even if we didn't have homework, we were supposed to read a book. Ugh! We had daily chores. We were expected to have good manners, to speak to adults politely, and, of course, never to talk back to grownups.

As teens we had curfews, and our parents always had to know where we were and with whom. There were some places we weren't allowed to go and other places we had to go—like church every Sunday. Life wasn't always full of rules, but as a kid I thought the balance leaned heavily in that direction. We had fun as a family. Vacations, picnics, walks and talks, and lots of hugs and *I love you*s, but I didn't appreciate them then.

Even when I began to have children of my own, I didn't think about Mother's wisdom; I was preoccupied with simply trying to get through each day! But as my kids grew and new challenges surfaced, I thought more and more about my mother and began to appreciate her in new ways.

My mom taught me many valuable lessons, but one sticks out in my mind. I must have been about seven when it happened. I had gone with Mom to a stationery store. I was free to wander up and down aisles that were filled with attractive, enticing items. There were more cards, pencils, pens, and notebooks than I'd ever seen! At my age, though, I was mesmerized by the huge bunches of brightly colored rubber bands. So many colors, so many bands! What fun it would be to have those, to be able to shoot them, to tie them together, to show them off to my brothers.

There are so many! I'm sure it would be okay if I took just one bunch. Nobody would even notice or care, I told myself.

Glancing over my shoulder to make sure nobody was looking, I slipped a bunch of the brightly colored bands into the pocket of my jacket. When I met my mother at the checkout counter, I tried hard to pretend that nothing was unusual.

We left the store, and I'm sure that my seven-year-old attempts to cover up only made me act a bit weird, arousing an observant mother's curiosity. At that time it seemed to me that my mother had eyes in the back of her head, some kind of a sixth sense or unusual intuitive knowledge that things weren't as they should be. Most moms don't miss much. Mine surely didn't!

Watching my awkward posture as I tried to cover my bulging pocket, my mother asked, "Susan, what are you doing? Is there something in your pocket?"

"No, Mommy," I replied.

Not to be fooled, my mother persisted. "I think there is. I

Susan in 1947 with her mother, Frances Alexander

want you to show me what it is."

Knowing I'd been found out, I carefully pulled the rubber bands out of my pocket and handed them to her. Her sad, angry look made me want to run away. But the worst was yet to come.

"Susan," she said, not mincing any words, "you took these without paying for them. That's stealing. You know that is wrong. We are going back to the store, and you will have to tell the manager what you have done and that you are sorry."

"I can't!" I wailed in utter embarrassment. "You take them in for me. I can't do that!"

"No," my wise mother replied. "You must do this. I will go with you, but you have to do it yourself."

Mom marched me back to the store and straight up to the manager's office, where I had to confess and apologize. The manager was understanding but stern as he looked me in the eye and said, "I hope you never steal anything again. I hope you have learned a lesson from this!"

At that moment a lesson was the farthest thing from my mind. I knew only that I was humiliated and so furious with my mother that I wanted to run away. The ride home was deadly silent.

It did not occur to me at the time that my mother was probably embarrassed too. I'm sure the last thing she wanted to do was to go all the way back to the store and deal with this. Certainly she had other things she needed to do. She could have dismissed this incident by just telling me that I had been wrong and that I shouldn't do such a thing again. She could have excused this, saying, "It's just a pack of rubber bands. I'll pay for them the next time I go in."

But she didn't. She was willing to be inconvenienced, to be humiliated, and to deal with her strong-willed child, who pitched a fit. Mom knew the importance of honesty. And she knew that teaching it must begin when we are young.

REFLECTION: *Am I willing to go out of my way to teach my child to be completely truthful and honest?*

Susan Alexander Yates is the mother of five: Allison Yates Gaskins, Chris, John, and twins Libby and Susy. She is also the proud grandmother of two. She is the author of *And Then I Had Kids, What Really Matters at Home,* and *How to Like the Ones You Love.* She is a columnist and speaker. She and her daughter Allison have written *Tightening the Knot* and *Thanks, Mom, for Everything.* Susan and her husband, John, live in Falls Church, Virginia, where he has pastored the Falls Church Episcopal Church for more than twenty years. Her daughter's essay, "Couches and White House Dinners," is next.

Allison Yates Gaskins
Daughter of Susan Alexander Yates

COUCHES AND
WHITE HOUSE DINNERS

*What is the bond between parent and child that can make the differ-
ence between citizens and criminals? It is the bond with the entwining
strands of love, praise, and discipline. Love is the emotional warmth
that gives us our security; praise is the word of pride or smile of approval
that gives us our self-worth; discipline is that consistently applied standard of right and wrong from which we get our moral values*

—David L. McKenna

When we were growing up, my brothers and sisters and
I always suspected that our mother was a little bit
crazy. Now that we're older, she seems to have regained most of
her senses, but for a while we wondered about her! One day in
particular stands out in my mind. I really questioned her sanity.
It was a Saturday afternoon in the fall, and Mom had been running errands all day. We five kids were raking leaves in the front
yard when Mom pulled into the driveway in our old beat-up
pickup truck. (It still amazes me that she wasn't embarrassed to
be seen in that thing.) As she leaped out of the truck, I noticed
something in the truck's bed.

"Hey, kids, come see what I got!" Mom yelled excitedly, and
we rushed over to investigate. We never knew what Mom would
be up to next. She climbed into the back of the truck, flung her
arms open wide, and cried, "Ta-da! Can you believe it was *free?*"
She wore an enormous smile of anticipation.

Climbing into the pickup to join her, we saw the ugliest couch
in the world. Once a blue-and-red plaid, but it was now faded
and stained, and the stuffing was coming out in spots.

"Mother, please tell me you're not putting *this* in the living room!" I groaned, dreading the embarrassment of explaining this monstrosity to my friends. Teenage boys were supposed to pull stunts like this, not mothers!

"Of course not!" Mom laughed and began to explain. "I'm going to put it in the garage. You see, I had this idea that we could clean out the garage a little bit and make it into a kids' hangout room. Mr. Larson down the street said we could have his old Ping-Pong table for only ten dollars if we wanted it, and we'll set that up in there too. Then, when friends come over you can hang out in the garage, stay up late, and not bother anybody! So what do you think?"

I looked at my brothers and sisters, who were obviously excited by the idea. "Hooray!" Chris yelled. "It can be a guys-only hangout. No girls allowed. Right, John?" John was quick to agree, but Mom interrupted as my sisters and I began to protest.

"You'll all share it. You know that's how we do things around here! But before we do anything else, we've got to get that garage cleaned out. Let's go!"

Rakes and leaf piles were deserted as we followed Mom to the garage. I had to admit, as crazy as Mom was to bring home a nasty couch, the idea of a hangout room was starting to grow on me. There was already a basketball hoop and a dartboard outside the garage. I wasn't so sure my girlfriends were into Ping-Pong, but at least we could sit on the couch (once I found a *clean* blanket to cover those spots) and talk.

Our garage quickly became a neighborhood favorite where kids in the neighborhood could relax, and Mom could not have been happier. She *loved* having lots of young people around the house. They all loved her too and treated her like one of the gang. Sometimes I would come home at night with friends and end up going to bed while Mom and my friends were still chatting! Everyone considered Mom his or her friend, and I was secretly very proud of having a "cool" mom.

Mom made our house always open to our friends, no matter who they were or what their background and reputation were. She loved everybody! Our parents were always very strict about our going out at night to parties and on dates, but Mom was always quick to remind us that we could always bring the party home! Her real concern was that we were safe. She was much happier knowing that the party was going on downstairs instead of somewhere else! I think that Mom and Dad probably passed many sleepless hours with Ping-Pong games and basketball tournaments going on outside their bedroom window at all hours of the night. But we never once heard them complain.

Mom wasn't the kind of mother who always had cookies and milk waiting for us. Instead she had refrigerated cookie dough, brownie mixes, and microwave popcorn available twenty-four hours a day. Even now, when my husband and I visit my parents, we can count on seeing my brothers and sisters and friends there in the kitchen! Sometimes, even when my siblings aren't there, their friends are. Mom has so endeared herself to them by her open heart and open-house policy that they know they can count on her to listen when no one else will. She made our home into one of love and acceptance for anyone who walked in our front door. (Oh, by the way, we still have that old couch in the garage. It's pretty much destroyed, but it's a very special monument to Mom's creative and thoughtful investment in our lives and our relationships.)

Another area where my mom was very involved in our lives as children was in developing our manners. Thursday nights were family nights in our household. We all had to be home for dinner no matter what. Baseball games, cheerleading practice, and church meetings were no excuse. You were there or else! On those nights we often had what Mom loved to call "White House dinners." No, our house was not white. In fact, it was red brick, and we lived on Broadmont Terrace instead of Pennsylvania Avenue.

But on Thursdays, it didn't matter where we were because we were eating at the White House. The President and First Lady never could make it to join us, but Mom and Dad stood in for them. Mom always argued, "You just never know when you might get invited someplace special for dinner. When you do, you'll be glad I taught you how to behave!"

There were many rules that we had to abide by at those White House dinners. Mom always cooked a "fancy" meal, and we set the table with the fine china, silver, and cloth napkins. We ate in the dining room instead of the kitchen, and Mom and Dad debated over just how dim the lights should be to get maximum "atmosphere" from the candles, while still allowing us to see the food on our plates. We all had to dress nicely, or at least put on a clean shirt and wash our faces. Mom always wore fresh lipstick, and Dad smelled good. We sat patiently at the table with our hands in our laps until Dad blessed the food (and he took an extra long time on Thursdays), thanked Mom for cooking such a lovely dinner, and began to serve the meal.

We passed everything to our right, served the person sitting next to us, took care to drop a little to the dog without letting

Allison as an infant with her mom, Susan Alexander Yates

Mom catch us, chewed with our mouths shut, and made sure our napkins were in our laps. If our elbows happened to graze the tablecloth, Mom would burst out in a rousing rendition of "Mabel, Mabel, strong and able, get your elbows off the table!" We were sure to have dish duty that night!

Mastering the intricacies of which spoon to use for soup and which for dessert, which knife belonged with the butter, and where to place your fork when you were finished was a complicated task requiring many, many Thursday nights at the White House. When the time finally came to clear the table, we were carefully instructed to ask politely, "Have you finished?" instead of "Are ya done?" (Only turkeys get "done," you know!), and we were cautioned against the greatest dinner *faux pas* of them all—stacking dishes at the table! Of course, even after everyone had finished eating, and our favorite television shows were well over, and we were all paralyzed from sitting up straight for so long, we *still* had to sit and make nice conversation while Mom and Dad drank bottomless cups of coffee. That was pure torture. Not even a telephone call was permitted to interrupt Mom's perfect White House dinners. Without fail we ate with the answering machine on.

After months and months of White House dinners, Mom decided that it was time to put us to the test. We would go out to a nice restaurant and see how well we could perform! Now, to us kids, this seemed like a much more reasonable way to learn manners than *pretending* we were at the White House. We figured that the First Family never had time for fancy dinners together anyway! So, we traipsed happily to the local Chinese restaurant, where we sat up tall and said "Please," "Thank you," and "Please pass the soy sauce" to perfection. Mom was definitely proud. She couldn't help but give us a few very specific reminders, though. Just as she was proclaiming vehemently in her not-so-quiet voice, "And remember, never, *ever* stack your plates. It's so rude!" our waiter, laden with a pile of dishes he had collected from another table, stepped up and asked, "Are ya done? Can I stack your plates?"

We all roared with laughter.

It took a few years and many more White House dinners for us to convince Mom that we were prepared for any glamorous occasion that might arise. And not too long ago, one actually did. We were all invited to the White House, the real one this time, for a holiday dinner party! And you know what? Thanks to Mom, we knew exactly what to do!

REFLECTION: *In what fun and creative ways can you be involved in your kids' lives? How will you use these fun times to instill values in your children?*

Allison Yates Gaskins is the mother of two, Caroline and Will. She and her husband, Will, live in Springfield, Virginia, where Will is a youth pastor. Allison enjoys reading, cooking, and taking walks. She has a special interest in foreign languages. She says that if she could do anything for enjoyment, she would study languages. Currently, she is taking a class in conversational French, just to stay proficient during these years when she is happily tied down with little ones. She and her mother have written two books: *Tightening the Knot* and *Thanks, Mom, for Everything.*

PART THREE

A Mother's Love

THE GREATEST OF THESE IS LOVE

God has chosen suffering as the avenue for perfecting His children. Let us not deny our children this grace.

—Edward L. Vardy

Jesus said, "Greater love has no one than this, that one lay down his life for his friends" (John 15:13 NIV). I can think of no one for whom I would give up my life more quickly than my child. A mother's love is fierce, loyal, protective, and self-sacrificing.

When my children were babies, I sometimes had dreams and nightmares about our family car being swept off a bridge, our house being broken into, or my child falling off a cliff on a family hike. Always in those dreams, I would be bravely and frantically fighting to save the babies and the littlest ones. Ashley has told me that she, too, is beginning to experience those frightening dreams and imaginings now that she is a mother. I believe it is a universal instinct among mothers to protect and rescue our children. We know intuitively and experientially that our children need us. Truly their survival depends on us.

Based on extensive studies he conducted over many years, psychoanalyst John Bowlby wrote about the importance of the mother-child bond in his book *Attachment.* He said, "The young child's hunger for his mother's love and presence is as great as his hunger for food." And by contrast, he went on to add, "Her loss or absence inevitably generates a powerful sense of loss and anger." [6]

God asked this question through the prophet Isaiah: "Can a mother forget the baby at her breast and have no compassion on the child she has borne?" (Isa. 49:15 NIV). The obvious answer is no. It is uncommon and unusual for a mother not to feel great love for the child she has birthed. God made women with a capacity to love our children with unending devotion.

But beyond the initial love affair a mother often feels for her newborns, beyond the heroic rescuing of her children from physical danger, what is it that keeps a mother lovingly devoted to her children for a lifetime? The knowledge that they will leave her someday and will need to make it on their own is what keeps a mother focused. She needs the ability to see into the future—to envision the finish line—because she knows it's up to her to prepare them for that life of independence. A mother knows from her own experience that the difficulties and insecurities of childhood will not last forever. A wise mother also knows that present difficulties, though unpleasant, are often the schoolroom for building character.

Love is not a feeling. If love were only and always a feeling, then there have been and still are many days when I do not love my children. Daily life has not been an easy road for me. It seems something always takes the edge off each day. I have battled allergies all of my life, with some days and seasons being worse than others. In my childbearing years, I was either tired from pregnancy or tired from nursing newborns at odd hours of the night and keeping up with the others. I think Lady Bird Johnson, wife of former President Lyndon Johnson, was speaking to me when she said, "Sometimes the greatest bravery of all is simply to get up in the morning and go about your business." On those hard-to-get-up mornings, I liked thinking I was brave in at least one area of my life.

And then, just as it seemed that I was reaching a place of respite with my youngest two in school, my older children had morphed into teenagers who wanted to stay up late at night to talk, to party, and to just hang with friends. Truly, it seems there is no rest for the weary mother. Motherhood is, as my husband said the other night, a season that begins but never ends.

Loving our children is not always natural, nor is it always easy. But it is absolutely essential. Mothers must love their children. A mother's constant love becomes the bedrock of security for her children. Before they leave home, there will be many times in their lives when it will seem to them that no one else loves them. Though they might wish for someone else's love, their mother's love will provide a North Star of security and hope in the midst of difficult days.

A favorite prayer (that I have prayed far more often than I ever imagined I would) goes like this:

> *Lord, help me to love my children as You do. Help me to see them as You do, to understand their needs as You do, to feel what they are feeling as You do. I cannot love my children as they need to be loved on my own. My children need Your love. I ask You to love my children through me.*

I have prayed this prayer most often for the sake of my teenagers—that they might not ever experience even a hint of rejection, disdain, or indifference from their mother.

The most poignant example of this in our family was when our son Samuel was in junior high school, a universally difficult time of life for most children. At age fourteen, Samuel was diagnosed with a form of muscular dystrophy, which had been slowly making itself evident in his body for two or three years. Over the next two years, he went from being a top-ranked tennis player and general all-around good athlete to a boy who was not able to run at all. His personality, which had always been delightful, playful, happy, and confident, changed to one of discouragement, anger, and hopelessness. Academics had never been his forte, but it didn't matter because he had athletics as a balance and an outlet. Now with his greatest strength suddenly changed to a weakness and a potentially life-altering one, school became a misery.

In the family, everyone grieved with him and wanted to help and be supportive. But no one grieved as my husband and I did. We understood the loss and felt its long-term implications better than anyone. His siblings had compassion, but only to a certain level, and only for so long.

As the process unfolded and reality sank in on us all, it seemed that life was going on for everyone but Samuel. And frankly, for the next two to three years, he was not very easy for people to like, let alone love. I often thought at the time that there was no one else on the planet who loved him but his dad and me. His teachers only saw the misbehavior and lack of achievement. His friends, in their own adolescent insecurities, only saw the kid who couldn't play basketball or baseball. His siblings usually only saw the brother who picked on them, or was mean to them, or who got Mom's and Dad's attention because of doctor visits.

The Raineys in 1991 at a neighborhood Christmas light display

Now, eight years or more since we first learned of his disease, we can look back and see how God has been at work in all our lives, but especially our son's. His lighthearted, life-of-the-party personality has returned. He has learned to use his disability to get people to laugh when he walks up on stage to emcee a college student discipleship meeting. He turned his love for tennis into a hard to beat Ping-Pong game. He has taught himself to play the guitar and has discovered an interest in leading worship music. But best of all is the greater tenderness to the Lord and to people that grew, and I believe will continue to grow, because of the things he suffered.

As we love our children, we must also remember that the Bible clearly teaches that "all who desire to live godly lives in Christ Jesus will suffer persecution" (2 Tim. 3:12 NKJV). In the midst of sufferings and trials, our children need our constant love and encouragement. They may need to borrow our faith and lean on our hope. But they don't always need us to rescue them and take away the distress. The thing that we want to fix may be the very thing God wants to use in their lives to build character and faith, which is what will last after we are gone.

Yes, a mother must love. She gives that love in spite of her child's rebellion, in spite of her child's unresponsiveness, in spite of her own circumstances. And there are a thousand other *in spite of*s that a mother must face in her lifetime as a mother. In them, she must find the ability to continue to love her child with the love that God gives.

A mother's relationship with her child begins with love, continues with love, and ends one day on earth with love. God's plan is for His children to know deep, abiding, unending love from at least one human being in their life, and that person is Mother.

A 24/7 MOM

Who but your mother shares your moments of glory? Who else sees you
at your weakest and most vulnerable and picks you up, helping you
grow strong? Your mom believes in your dreams, even when they lie
in tatters at your feet. She picks you up and helps you dream again.
         —Brenda Hunter and Holly Larson
            In the Company of Friends

A full-time mom spends around 8,000 hours with her kids each year, according to my estimation! That means that from my birth to the time I left home for college at age eighteen, my mom logged about 144,000 hours with me. I started thinking about all that my mom has given me during those years of my life, and I am amazed. She hasn't done it alone, but it has been her full-time job.

Until I became a mom last year, I worked full-time with a local ministry. After my son was born, people would ask me if I was still working. I would reply, "I quit my *part*-time job at the ministry, and now have a *full*-time job with no holidays, no vacations, and no overtime pay."

I usually got a laugh from that, but it is true. As a full-time mom, you are on call 24 hours a day, 7 days a week, 365 days a year. And this goes on until that child is out on her own, about 18 to 24 years later. Then you may not be on call 24/7, but you're still a mom, and that's if you just have one child. For my mom it will be another four years before she is an empty nester. What an investment she has made.

How did she do it? She accomplished it one day at a time. My mom was there for all the little things, which, when added together, equal a lifetime of impact that no one else could have.

She was there when I took my first steps. She was there when I said my first words. When I started public school in the sixth grade, she was there to walk with me to my first class. When I came home from school in the afternoon with homework and questions, she was there. In junior high when I tried out for cheerleading and didn't make it, she was there. She was there for the next few years of practicing at the gym once a week and at home so I could reach my dream of being a cheerleader. When I tried out again in high school and finally made it, she was there.

When I tested my boundaries by meeting a guy at the mall after I had been told not to, she was there to come alongside me and inflict punishment (in love, of course). When we had science-fair projects, she would stay up many times until after midnight, working on them with us. When we got ready for school in the mornings, she was there, making pancakes or oatmeal and helping us pack our lunches. When I cheered at games, she came to watch and cheer me on. When I wanted to start a Bible study after school, she was the one who came to help me lead and develop my vision for others. She was there when our kittens were born and my bunny died. She was the one we went to when we were sick. She was there every morning to pray for us as she drove us to school.

In addition to providing us with daily support, encourage-

Ashley's first steps (1975)

ment, and direction, Mom started some wonderful holiday traditions when we were kids. Our family spent every Thanksgiving for ten years in Colorado because my Dad's ministry held a conference there and he was the speaker. Because we stayed in a condo without all the capabilities of a full kitchen needed for the traditional turkey dinner, the only meal we could eat together on Thanksgiving Day was breakfast. Mom began a tradition of a special family brunch. During our breakfast Mom would read to us about the Pilgrims: how they came to and settled in the New World, and how during much of the second winter they all lived on a daily ration of five kernels of corn, yet no one died of starvation.[7] So each year we began our brunch with five kernels of corn on our plates. We shared the things we're thankful for, one item per kernel. We wrote them down so that we would be reminded of what we were most thankful for that year. After breakfast, we'd all go skiing together. We don't go to Colorado anymore, but we still have brunch together before we head out to my grandparents' farm to eat a real turkey dinner with our extended family.

At Christmastime Mom taught us how to make homemade butter cookies. We'd bake all day and then decorate them. I remember loving those times with my mom. Now I've invested in cookie cutters for every holiday so I can make those special cookies. I have to admit that I haven't been as faithful to make them, except at Christmas, but then that's the tradition. Mom was able to spend time preparing for those special holidays and involving us because she was home every day. Through her creative ideas, she made the holidays a time of hope and excitement. I look forward to passing on those fun experiences to my children.

But beyond the traditions and ball games, birthday parties, and school projects, Mom showed me the greatest kind of love and devotion by just being there every day. I never had to wonder where she was. I never came home to an empty house. When she had to travel with my dad, I knew it wasn't permanent. Don't get me wrong; we didn't get everything we wanted as kids. But, looking back, I don't feel deprived of those things I missed out on because my mom didn't work. We had stability in our lives because she was there. That's something you can't put a price tag on.

Now I see what a profound impact her presence has had on me as a woman, as a wife, and as a mother. Because she was there I learned what it looks like to be a mom who takes delight in her children and in her role as a wife. I saw her greet my father at the end of each day, and I saw in their marriage the roles God intended: wife-helper, husband-leader. I learned to view life through God's eyes, because that's how my mom taught me to look at life. I wanted to be like her, and I still do (I think all little girls want to be like their moms). After God and my husband, Michael, I want my family to be my priority.

There are a lot of hours in a year and even in a day that you can spend with your children. As a mom the single greatest gift you can give them is your time, which speaks love and conveys devotion louder than anything else. Be there for your children if you can. It's a sacrifice you won't regret! Someone will impact your child today—will it be you?

Ashley, Rebecca, and Laura
making Christmas cookies in 1987

Nancy Leigh DeMoss
Daughter of Nancy Sossomon DeMoss

---------- ◀┼ ----------

DEVOTION TO FAMILY

Nobody appreciates mothers more than their single daughters. When asked to name the one person who loved them most and knew them intimately, single women invariably named their mothers.

—Carin Fubenstein
adapted from *New Woman*

*O*n November 30, 1957, Arthur DeMoss and Nancy Sossomon exchanged their wedding vows. Within a week, the nineteen-year-old bride was expecting her first child. Within the first five years of their marriage, my parents had six children. (A seventh followed some years later.) Though this was not according to their original plans (they had planned to wait five years to have children!), they gladly embraced each child as a gift from God.

Life was never again to be uneventful for this young Southern girl who had married a man thirteen years her senior. Converted to Christ at the age of twenty-four, Art DeMoss was sold out to the Lord and intended to make every moment of his life count for eternity.

As the firstborn child of this consecrated couple, I have been blessed to bear the name and many of the characteristics of a remarkable woman. My mother's example has shaped how I view my calling as a woman, how I relate to men, and, most importantly, how I relate to my heavenly Bridegroom, the Lord Jesus.

As I was growing up, I didn't realize that my mother's view of her role as a wife and mother was terribly out of sync with our times. In many ways her lifestyle was politically incorrect, since she saw the deceptive, destructive nature of the world's concept of "liberated womanhood." Instead she chose to pattern her life after the One who refused to live independently of His Father and who delighted to do the will of the One who sent Him.

Though an extraordinarily gifted woman in her own right, my mother willingly laid down a promising career as a sacred vocalist to be a suitable helper to her husband.

My dad's lifestyle, though exciting and challenging, was also complex and demanding. In the climate of the sixties, where women were encouraged to pursue independence, careers, personal recognition, and self-satisfaction, my mother modeled a different role—one in which a woman adapts to the heart and calling of her husband. Rather than expecting her husband's life to revolve around her needs and interests, her life revolved around her husband's.

Art DeMoss was a visionary. He was always full to the brim with new ideas—whether in his business or in the greatest passion of his life—to reach more people with the gospel. Whenever he had another dream, my mother was always there to cheer him on, to encourage him, and to help make that dream become a reality.

In the early days, my dad dreamed of selling insurance through direct-mail marketing. Mother worked with him at the kitchen table in their apartment to design the ads, write the letters, and

Nancy Leigh DeMoss with her mother, Nancy Sossomon DeMoss

process the responses. He also dreamed of inviting business and professional men and women to dinner to hear a gospel presentation—first a small handful, then scores, hundreds, and ultimately thousands. She maintained the lists of names and addresses, and she sent out the invitations. The day of each event she supervised the meal preparation and service, stood by his side to greet the guests (he depended on her incredible gift of remembering names), and stayed up to put the house back together long after the guests left and the family went to bed.

It is important to understand that this helper role was not something my dad demanded of my mother; neither was it a position that she accepted grudgingly or reluctantly. She truly adored this man and found delight in walking through life as his partner and encourager.

Mother gladly managed the domestic affairs of a very active household so he could be free to better fulfill God's call for his life. Many women today would consider this lifestyle oppressive. But my mother was far from downtrodden. To the contrary, my father cherished and highly esteemed the partner God placed by his side, and he was delighted to see her maximize her God-given potential and abilities.

In the rough-and-tumble world of business, my father was not without his detractors, but he could always count on my mother being his number-one admirer. To this day, I can never remember her speaking negatively about him to us or to anyone else. It's not that he didn't have some glaring weaknesses (though she sometimes gives that impression!), but rather that she was scarcely conscious of the negatives because of her deep, genuine admiration for him.

My dad had some idiosyncrasies that many wives would have considered obsessive or intolerable. For example, he was compulsive about cleanliness, about not being disturbed while sleeping or napping, and about eating three meals a day at precisely the same time. He had peculiar dietary restrictions and had little or no aptitude for domestic or mechanical matters. In each of these areas, I remember my mother simply adapting to his ways, without making issues out of what are truly insignificant matters in the big picture.

Though their backgrounds were quite different, my mother supported my father by upholding the standards he established for our home. I realize now that they could not have had identical views on every issue, but rarely were we conscious of any disagreements about our family's basic values and practices.

My mother considered it the highest honor to be Mrs. Arthur DeMoss. By her example, she taught me to be attentive and tuned to the needs of the men in my sphere of influence—to respect and honor them, and to joyfully serve them and place their needs ahead of my own.

My mother imparted to me a vision of a woman being a cheerleader for the men in her life. Her example has caused me to look for ways, even as a single woman, to be an encourager and to accentuate the godly qualities in the lives of pastors, Christian leaders, and the men I serve alongside in ministry. It has given me the wisdom to counsel women with difficult husbands to make allowances for their husband's rough edges and to verbalize only his positive qualities to others.

Above all, her model has led me to reverence, honor, and joyously obey the Lord Jesus, the supreme love of my life. I long to be attentive to Him, to serve Him, to fulfill His wishes, to be by His side, and to let others know of my deep admiration for Him. These longings were first planted in my heart from the heart of my mother.

REFLECTION: *What lessons about the role of women are you teaching your daughter? Does she see a positive example in the way you relate to your husband or father?*

A native of Philadelphia, **Nancy Leigh DeMoss** grew up in a family that was deeply committed to Christ and to the mission of world evangelization. At an early age she surrendered her life to Christ and to His call to serve in His kingdom.

Nancy graduated from the University of Southern California with a degree in piano performance. After college she served on the staff of a large church in the area of children's ministries. Since 1980 Nancy has served as the Director of Publications and Women's Ministries and as editor of *Spirit of Revival* magazine for Life Action Ministries, a revival ministry based in Niles, Michigan.

Toni Britt Fortson
Daughter of Sarah Elizabeth Britt

—◄—

SERVING AS JESUS DID

*Just as the Son of Man did not come to be served, but to serve,
and to give his life as a ransom for many.*

—Matthew 20:28 NIV

$\mathcal{M}$y mother was born in 1923. Her father worked multiple jobs to provide for and feed his sixteen children and his wife. He was employed by a local oil company, worked for the railroad, and was a farmer out of necessity. My mother was the ninth child in a family of five boys and eleven girls. Her mother, my grandmother, took in laundry to help with the family income, but most of her time was devoted to caring for the needs of such a full quiver. She was a resourceful woman who could cook a meal beyond your imagination, as well as sew clothes by hand that looked like they had been sewn by machine (she could not afford a sewing machine in those days). To this very day I have a baby dress and sweater handmade by my grandmother for me when I was an infant. The tiny hand stitching is, amazingly, almost perfect; the sweater and dress are priceless treasures.

My mother grew up learning the importance of helping, sharing, and serving. With a family the size of hers, family fun was centered around holidays, birthdays, and Sundays. Special foods were prepared, and joy and laughter were present at many bountiful feasts. My grandmother was the spiritual leader because my grandfather was often at work, which many times took him away from home. I can remember my grandmother singing hymns and always talking about God's goodness whenever we (my sister, my brother, and I) would visit their humble little house in Swedesboro, New Jersey.

Because of the heavy responsibilities of helping at home, and especially after her father died when she was fifteen, my mother didn't have the opportunity to finish her education. About six years after she married my father (when I was in first grade), she took a job in the home of a doctor and nurse who had six children. There she did much of what she had been doing most of her life—giving herself to meet the needs of others. She became a very important part of this family while still maintaining her own family.

In Mother's early days of working for this family, their young children often came to her with their needs, whether the need was a sandwich for lunch or first aid for a skinned knee. Mother treated them as if they were her own children. After taking care of their physical needs, she told them about Jesus and how He loved and cared for them. Sometimes they laughed, but sometimes they listened.

As they became older and more influenced by their peers, they responded to her godly wisdom with jokes and ridicule. Mother never let this bother her, and she kept right on serving that family until all the children were grown and on their own. Her life and the godly wisdom she shared from day to day penetrated each child. One accepted Christ, and is currently involved in Christian ministry with her husband. Years later this woman wrote a letter to Mother, thanking her for being bold enough to share her faith with their family during her growing-up years,

Sarah Britt, mother of Toni Britt
Fortson, at age seventy-five
ᐯ

and telling her how God had used Mother to show her as a child her need for salvation.

My mother's life taught us serving. An essential part of my grandmother's life was meeting the physical needs of others as she shared the love of Jesus and hope in life with Christ, and she passed that on to my mother. Now I am a mother of three, and this heritage of service has become part of my daily life. I used to struggle with this gift of serving because, as an African American woman, I knew my people often had little choice other than to serve. But God has shown me that service is a great gift which He holds in high esteem, as evidenced by the fact that Jesus came to serve mankind. If the Son of God could serve humanity and even go so far as to die on the cross for my sins and yours, I surely must not let Satan rob me of the joy of such a heavenly opportunity. Yes, African Americans served this country without choice for the most part, but I am not ashamed of the contribution that we made, and I choose to use it today as a way of bringing honor to my Savior, who showed me how to do it by His grace.

When I think of my mother's influence on my life, I have to give her credit for teaching me to serve, as Jesus did: "The greatest among you will be your servant" (Matt. 23:11 NIV).

Toni Britt Fortson

Toni Britt Fortson is the mother of three: Sheila, Joya, and Tommy. She graduated from the University of Michigan and is a homemaker. She enjoyed homeschooling all three of her children for eighteen years. Toni has been a Family Life Conference speaker with her husband for the past ten years. She lives in Denver, Colorado, with her husband, Tom, who is executive vice president of Promise Keepers. Her daughter's essay is "Virtue and Femininity."

Mary Jenson
Daughter of Missy Kunz

—+—

LOVE IS PATIENT

Who is getting more pleasure from this rocking, the baby or me?
—Nancy Thayer

*U*nderneath Mom's new Nancy Reagan wig was a bald head I hadn't yet seen. Her smart clothes had been left behind. Shuffling down the airport corridor with my sister, she looked like someone else's elderly mother, slower in step and with a dimness that belied her natural enthusiasm. I couldn't fling my arms around her neck and start my customary nonstop chatter; nor could I sneak up behind her and surprise her as I might have in the past. For the first time in my life she was fragile, porcelain, opalescent.

Waving to give plenty of warning, I walked toward them, willing the moisture out of my eyes. "Hi, you sweet thing." I put my arms around her. My sister and I exchanged knowing looks, the kind mothers share over their children's heads. And so began our last four months together.

Mom came to my California home the summer of 1990 to give my sisters a respite from her care, and to help me understand what she and they were going through. It was an eye-opener. Her non-Hodgkin's lymphoma had recently spread undetected to her brain. There it pushed aside short-term memory and the ability to perform certain habitual tasks we take for granted.

Numerous little oddities defined each day. Mom set the table with three forks at this place, two knives and a spoon at that one. She poured orange juice into the coffee thermos and wrapped drippy watermelon in paper towels to store in the refrigerator.

Just getting her dressed became a group activity.

Everything we did that summer took longer than I thought it would. Mom gave simple tasks the same weight as weekend forays to the mountains. I wrestled with my impatience, astonished and embarrassed that my mother could elicit from me any emotion other than affection. One morning as we were running late again (and I was mentally tapping my foot), a phrase I'd heard recently came to mind: "Love is slow." I'm told that it came from a small boy who was rushed from one activity to another by his equally hurried mom. When he was asked the "simple" question "What is love?" he had replied, "Love is slow."

That phrase became my mantra for those summer weeks that marked the beginning of the end of our sweet on-earth relationship. Upon reflection, I realized that it was that same kind of slow, patient love that was my mother's greatest gift to me. She had spent so much time with me in my childhood, and now I needed to give her that same steady, patient love.

Mom's "slow love" was manifested in the fact that we could talk at length about everything—and all at once—for as long as we needed. Our conversations flitted back and forth from the serious to the superficial. For Christmas one year I found a mug with a slogan that began, "All I really want out of life are world peace and thin thighs." It seemed to encapsulate the breadth and depth of our slow, easy discussions, and though the concluding sentence was totally trivial ("Actually I don't care that much

Missy Kunz, mother
of Mary Jenson

about world peace"), I loved giving it to her because she, too, appreciated the comfortable range of our communication.

One morning that last summer, as I agonized over my short responses to her, she said to me, "Honey, being with you is like putting on a comfortable old shoe." *I felt* like an old shoe, yet not a very comfortable one, after that compliment.

I often think of the mornings she got up at 5:00, uncomplaining, to set my hair in those prickly brush rollers. And then I remember the nights she sat on my bed, talking, scratching my back for as long as she could stay awake. I remember the softness of her skin on mine, the way her hand would slow to a stop as she'd nod sleepily over my back, and the way I could get her moving again by flinching in a nonchalant sort of way, as if in restlessness rather than demand.

I remember the nights she sat up with my first child and me, rocking with us in the dark. She told me his milky sighs smelled like angel breath—and I remember my sense of panic and abandonment when she had to leave.

She's the only one in my life then or now who was interested in everything about me—or at least made me think she was. I still catch myself reaching for the phone to tell her something important or funny—or scanning my list of friends for one tolerant enough to hear the trifling details of my life.

What a gift to leave one's children—the knowledge that your time is theirs, and they are the focus of your attention. Child psychologist Dr. Urie Bronfrenbrenner was once asked, "What is the key ingredient in the successful development of a human being?" Without hesitation he replied, "Someone, some adult, has to be crazy about the kids." Mom showed me that she was crazy about me by being slow and deliberate.

I was forty-one years old when Mom died—too young to lose a mother. Now, nine years later, I can't hear her voice in my mind anymore. That disturbs me. My memory of her face, sustained by photographs, is still clouded by the last weeks of her life, when her eyes were blank and her skin lifeless, like a peach past its freshness. But when I think of her, it's not her physical image that's important to me.

I think of the banter, the friendship, the way she routinely ended our phone calls with, "Bye, honey. I love you." I remember shopping with her, sitting together and talking with our feet stretched out in front of us, laughing so hard at the same joke that we'd have to leave the room to breathe.

And I feel her presence when I wrap my arms around my chil-

Mary with her mother and children at the swimming pool

dren, as she did around me, and when I, too, scratch backs and talk late into the night. I recognize her words in my own conversation. Some women say with regret, "I'm becoming my mother." Not me. I long to be more like my mother. But though I can't duplicate her life or personality, I hope I'm passing on to my children her gift of slow love.

Adaptations of this article have been printed in *A Tribute to Moms* (Multnomah, 1997) and *Still Life* (Multnomah, 1997).

Mary Jenson is the mother of two grown children, Matt and Molly. She credits her mother, Missy Kunz, with showing her an uncompromising, unequaled, unconditional, unflappable, undying love. She is the author of *Partners in Promise* and *Still Life*. She is a recent empty nester and says that while she's happiest living a hermit's life, she does enjoy joining her husband, Ron, in speaking for FamilyLife conferences. She and her husband live in San Diego, California. Her daughter's essay, "A Gift to God," is next.

Molly Jenson with her mother, Mary Kunz Jenson

—←—

A GIFT TO GOD

It will be gone before you know it. The fingerprints on the wall
appear higher and higher. Then suddenly they disappear.
—Dorothy Evslin

From birth to high school I was very attached to my mother. Like most children, I felt she was the only one who could comfort me. Many days in elementary school, junior high, and even high school I missed school because of a faked illness; I just wanted to be home with my mom. I would freak out when she would leave on trips, even short ones, because I knew she wouldn't be there to quiet my angst. I would run to her when I had a stomachache, when I stubbed my toe, or when someone made fun of me at school. Her touch calmed my fears. And she always knew how to get my mind off the bad things and onto the good. She was the only one who could comfort me—or so I thought.

When I was twelve, my mom went on a trip for two weeks. She knew I would panic (which I did to the extreme), so before she left she got out her Bible and showed me a verse that I now hold dear to my heart: "No temptation has seized you except what is common to man. And God is faithful; he will not let you be tempted beyond what you can bear. But when you are tempted, he will also provide a way out so that you can stand up under it" (1 Cor. 10:13 NIV).

Mother told me to read this verse whenever I felt sick, missed her, or was fearful in any way. That verse showed me that I wasn't alone, and I wasn't the only one who had problems. And although I thought my problems were insurmountable, 1 Corinthians 10:13 reassured me that I was pretty well off and that I really had nothing to worry about. I memorized that verse while my mom was gone and said it over and over in my head.

Until I was twelve I had never really thought of God as tangible. I didn't expect to touch or to see Him, but I also didn't know I could ever feel Him. Yet *I felt* Him when I read that verse. His indescribable peace and comfort passed through me. I never knew that there was greater love than the sweet autumn eyes and soothing touch of my mom, yet our Holy God of comfort cared enough about me to put my worries at ease. The day Mom left on her two-week trip, she showed me the One who could answer all my problems, the King of all comfort—God, *Jehovah-shalom*, the Lord of peace, my heavenly Father. I didn't need to depend on my mother for support or assurance. I had God and His holy Word to run to whenever my burdens were heavy.

As I write this, I realize why I wanted to share these ever-so-cherished memories of my childhood. It isn't because my mom showed me the importance of the Scriptures, but because my mother gave me a gift that both scares me and excites me. A gift I am going to give my children someday. The hardest gift any mother can give. She gave me away. She gave me to God. She showed me where her greatest hope lay, and in that simple gesture she gave me back to the One who gave me to her.

REFLECTION: *Have you given your children to God?*

Molly Jenson is the daughter of Mary and Ron Jenson. She attended Point Loma Nazarene University and was recruited to sing for a contemporary youth praise band, Everybodyduck. Traveling with this band is one of her lifelong dreams. Molly also enjoys photography and is currently working with her dad on a writing project about dads and daughters.

A Mother's Love

Mothers fill places so great that there isn't an angel in heaven who wouldn't be glad to give a bushel of diamonds to come down here and take their place.

—Billy Sunday

My mother showed me her love in these unforgettable ways:

_____

_____

_____

_____

I want to show my love to my children in these special ways:

_____

_____

_____

_____

When all is said, it is the mother only who is a better citizen than the soldier who fights for his country. The successful mother, the mother who does her part in rearing and training aright the boys and girls, who are to be the men and women of the next generation, is of greater use to the community, and occupies, if she only would realize it, a more honorable, as well as more important, position than any man in it. The mother is the one supreme asset of the national life. She is more important, by far, than the successful statesman, or business-man, or artist, or scientist.

—Teddy Roosevelt (1858–1919)

Barbara Rosberg
Daughter of Colleen Bedford

ALWAYS THERE FOR ME

A mother is the truest friend we have, when trials, heavy and sudden, fall upon us: when adversity takes the place of prosperity; when friends who rejoice with us in our sunshine, desert us when troubles thicken around us, still will she cling to us, and endeavor by her kind precepts and counsels to dissipate the clouds of darkness, and cause peace to return to our hearts.

—Washington Irving (1783–1859)

*C*hildhood memories. When I think of my younger years, numerous heartwarming thoughts run through my head. Many of those thoughts include stories of my mother and me. Her beauty, her womanhood, her love, her companionship, her devotion, her sacrifice, her understanding, and, most of all, her prayers, fill my thoughts as I reminisce about my mother and my little-girl days. Let me tell you about my mother, Colleen Bedford, and her impact on my life.

Her beauty. One Mother's Day when I was six, my dad bought a gold convertible. A gift for my mom, he said, but I always knew that car had a special place in *his* heart. She was free-spirited at the wheel of the convertible, listening to "Alley Cat" on the radio and pumping the brakes to make the car "dance" to the rhythm of the music! She wore a smile on her face and a scarf around her head so her hair wouldn't blow in the wind. On some days, if it got too windy, she'd leave the windows up when the top was down. In embarrassment my older brother and I would duck. Yet even as she dodged the wind-blown look and drove a car that danced to "Alley Cat," I was so proud of my mother. She was blonde, blue-eyed, petite—a beautiful woman and a fashion model to top it off, the most beautiful homeroom mother any kid could have. And her brains matched her beauty. During World War II she worked at the Pentagon, placing civilians with overseas employment while Dad served our country in the Marines.

Her womanhood. When I was a preschooler, my mom and I had matching pink mother-daughter dresses. She would dress me in that dress, black patent leather shoes, lacy white cotton socks, and white gloves, and we would go to the tearoom with her friends for lunch and a style show. I still remember sitting in a youth chair at those elegant tables, beaming from ear to ear. A hostess would come over and open a wooden sewing box and offer me a party favor, a gift wrapped in white tissue.

Her love. As a little girl I loved our walks, hand in hand, in Greenwood Park behind our town's art center. She poured her life into mine. That one-on-one time with her spelled L-O-V-E to me, a kid too young yet to spell.

Her companionship. One of my favorite activities was swinging on the swing set in that park with her. I'd sit on her lap, facing her and watch her rear back and laugh with the sun shining on her radiant face. Her stiffly styled hair would blow as we went backward and forward, and it would make me giggle. Oh, the wonderful smell of my mom— a combination of beauty cream and Joy perfume.

Her devotion. Nothing was as important to my mom as her family. How did I know that? Because each day as I left for school, her words resonated in my heart as she cried out, "I love you, Barbie! Have a good day. I'm praying for you!" I echoed the same heartfelt love back to her as she closed the door behind me.

Her sacrifice. My mother always said that those days with

preschoolers were the longest days yet the shortest years. She valued my life so much that she stayed home with me and put her career on hold until later. Nothing competed with her kids. She was the kind of mother who kept me home when I was sick, and she was considerate in keeping me out an extra day so that other kids wouldn't get sick. Deep down I knew that Mother just loved having me home. It met my need, and it met hers too. My femininity and womanhood are tied to my mother's blue eyes. Those blue eyes have reminded me that my life is a miracle.

Her understanding. The most important memory I have of my mom is the feeling of her understanding me. Once when she was gone for a week, someone in the neighborhood yelled at me, and I ran home. I took my dad into my parents' bedroom and whispered through my tears what had happened. But he was confused and didn't understand. I attempted to tell my grandmother, too. It was then that I knew I not only missed Mom, but also that I needed her. She always was soothing and tender, allowing me time to cry.

Her prayers. How did she have the energy to comfort an emotional little girl? She prayed! How do I know? I would sneak over and open the door to our upstairs and watch her weep and pray

The Bedford Family— Colleen, Barbara, Barry, and Jack

◄✦

at the top of those stairs in front of the picture of Jesus. I'd whisper to my brother, "She's praying again." For nineteen years I depended on her prayers, because until I was that old, I really didn't know how prayer fit into God's plan for me. There, in that very room at the top of the stairs, sitting in front of the picture of Jesus, my brother Barry prayed with me, and I finally realized my need for God and asked Him to become my Lord. Because of that I now know how to listen for the voice of our heavenly Father as I go into my closet and kneel and pray for my own family.

Children need their mothers during those early years, but remember that it's critically important for us as mothers to stay connected to our children for a lifetime! Few roles on this earth demand that we lay down our lives for a lifetime, putting aside the things that can distract us. Yet it's in giving up that we get back so much more! When we fully embrace our roles as mothers, our hearts are developed in ways that no other life experience could teach us! And if we are surrendered to God and obedient to the task, in time our lives reflect the very sacrificial nature of God. Now it doesn't get any better than that, does it? So here's to you, Mom. If you ever wondered if you made a difference in my life, now you surely know you did! I love you!

 **Barbara Rosberg** is the mother of two daughters, Sarah and Missy, and the "mom-in-law" of Sarah's husband, Scott. She and her husband, Gary, coauthored the book *Guard Your Heart.* Barbara graduated from Drake University. She speaks nationally, cohosts a syndicated radio show with Gary, and is the vice president of America's Family Coaches, the ministry she serves with her husband. The Rosbergs live in West Des Moines, Iowa. Her daughter's essay, "Love, No Matter What," is next.

Missy Rosberg
Daughter of Barbara Rosberg

—⊷—

LOVE NO MATTER WHAT

The heart of a mother is a deep abyss at the bottom of which you will always find forgiveness.

—Honoré de Balzac (1799–1850)

*L*ove is patient, love is kind. It does not envy, it does not boast, it is not proud. It is not rude, it is not self-seeking, it is not easily angered, it keeps no record of wrongs. Love does not delight in evil but rejoices with the truth. It always protects, always trusts, always hopes, always perseveres. Love never fails." (1 Cor. 13:4–8 NIV)

Has anyone ever told you they'd love you no matter what? No matter what you've done or will do, they'd love you just the same? My mom has always said that. I'd hear it and wonder, *Can she really love me no matter what?* That kind of love is called unconditional love; it is the kind of love Jesus gave us and continues to give us every second of every day. That's the origin of "love keeps no record of wrongs" (1 Cor. 13:5). Reading that, I am reminded of the time that my mother proved to me that she meant what she said.

More than four years ago I was a freshman in high school. I'm amazed when I look back and see how much I've grown since then. I liked people, liked boys, liked to have fun, and *didn't* like to focus on school. Everyone I knew walked around feeling overwhelmed that it was finally our freshman year at Valley High School. That year was *the* year for me. I had all the friends in the world, an older boyfriend who was the varsity basketball star, and never-ending activities on weekends.

I'd come home from a party and my older sister, Sarah (then a senior), would be sitting at home watching television. I'd tell her to go out and have fun and quit staying home on the weekends. "You're a senior!" I'd say.

I was a moral girl who grew up in a strong Christian home, yet I was embarrassed to tell people about my faith. I'd go to the parties and choose not to drink because I knew it was wrong, but I didn't really know *why* it was wrong. I've always been a strong person, but the strength I had then was not really strength, since I was holding on to my own strength. I quickly learned how weak I was.

I started making mistakes. I wasn't doing anything outlandishly wrong, but my mistakes were more about compromise and the positions I allowed myself to be in. Most of all, my relationship

Barbara and Missy Rosberg on Missy's prom night

with God was slacking. I was no longer the joyful, bouncy Missy everyone was used to. Instead I was turning into the adolescent who couldn't figure out who she was, and in the process was trying to be like everyone else. I was trying to ignore the fact that I had Jesus in my heart. Because of that, I knew I had it all, and yet it wasn't good enough for me. I kept running faster and faster until I couldn't run anymore. Then I hit rock bottom.

I can't quite remember how it happened or exactly when it was. I was in my room late one night feeling empty and hurt. Everyone around me was repeatedly letting me down. My friends were frustrating me, my boyfriend had broken up with me, and I felt alone. But my mom was there. She was sitting next to me on my bed; it was one of those nights that I made my mom come in my room and listen to everything I had to say. She'd listen, and I'd talk. Then she'd talk, and I'd listen! (She has always been the best listener and I've always been a talker, but when she opens her mouth, I know it's my time to listen!)

I can remember that night as if it were last night. As we were sitting there talking, something made me open up and tell her everything I had been hiding all year. All the things I was hurting about and keeping inside of me, the things that brought my smile to a frown each day. I told her the little things; I told her the big things. To most people my age, those things weren't a big deal, but to me they were huge sins that were pulling me down. If sins are pulling you away from Christ, they're big.

As my mom listened to me that night, she didn't say what I feared she would say. She didn't tell me she was disappointed in me. She didn't ground me. She told me instead that I had already been forgiven, long before that night. Not only was I forgiven, but those sins were also forgotten—by Jesus *and* by my mom. She could have handled it any way she wanted, but she decided to handle it the way Christ would want her to. She proved to me that true love doesn't keep any record of wrongs. If you love someone, you can look past their flaws and their past and forgive them. From that day on, I was reminded that my mom was not only a woman of her word, but also a godly woman who knew the true meaning of unconditional love.

My mom is my best friend and my sister in Christ. The Bible says, "Love covers a multitude of sins" (Prov. 10:12, author's paraphrase), and I've learned that is true. Mom fails me and I fail her daily, but God covers all our failures with His love. Someday I will be able to thank my God face to face for His love and sacrifice for me. But for now I want to thank my mom for the love she gives me each day, each hour. Through each accomplishment and failure, she still loves me. Thank you, Mom, for your love. And thank You, Jesus, for my mom!

REFLECTION: *What might your teenage daughter write about you? Even though your child may only be a preschooler, your relationship now is the foundation of the friendship that will come.*

Missy Rosberg is a communications major at Bethel College and Seminary in St. Paul, Minnesota. She enjoys swing dancing and does not mind "making a sacrifice" to enjoy her dancing, like going to her prom all decked out in a formal dress but wearing tennis shoes to be able to quickly execute the intricate steps. Missy is the daughter of Gary and Barb Rosberg, founders of America's Family Coaches.

Photo © Thomas & Bruce Photography, Des Moines, Iowa

Sheryl Lemon (in front) with her sisters—Sandra, Lisa (infant),
and Kathy—and mother, Helen

Sheryl Lemon Wunder
Daughter of Helen Smith Lemon

—◂+—

ACROSS THE GENERATIONS

When I stopped seeing my mother with the eyes of a child, I saw the woman who helped me give birth to myself.
—Nancy Friday in *My Mother, Myself*

    I sit here looking at a black-and-white photograph of my mother, her face young and fresh. At her feet are her four young daughters, all wearing cotton pinafores. I can remember how the stiffly starched ruffles, which ran down our backs like angel wings, took my mom hours to iron on a humid Southern morning.

I miss the companionship of my mother. She died of leukemia twelve years ago. If we could be together again, I would thank her for the wonderful lesson about motherhood—a powerful influence subtly conveyed—she gave to me. Though some lessons are simply life moments stumbled upon, the importance of committed motherhood was a lesson my mother taught throughout her life. But for years I took for granted her quiet, immense devotion to her role.

Simple events built my child's view of who my mother was and what she did. To my four-year-old ears, the loud gurgle of water as it rushed down the kitchen-sink drain was terrifying, and it sounded strong enough to take me with it. So after my nightly bath in the sink, my mom helped me step carefully out, naked and dripping, before she pulled the plug. I can remember how her side of the bed smelled—warm and safe—when I streaked there during a frightening thunderstorm. We made frequent visits to see her mother and sister; they would sit on the porch glider during the thickly warm Southern nights, drinking tea and talking about various family members and neighbors. My cousins and I would slip onto the porch quietly, hoping not to be noticed and then banished from the grownups' presence.

When I was a little girl, my mother combed my unruly auburn tangles and told me how beautiful my hair was. By the time I was in seventh grade, my hair grew coarse and snarled in unmanageable curls, and I didn't know what to do with it. My mother finally suggested, "Maybe if we set curls in your hair with bobby pins, that might help."

I thought this sounded very old-fashioned and refused, but my resourceful mom determinedly tried again. "Why don't you try rolling your hair on brush rollers like your older sister?" That sounded more modern and appealing, so I agreed, and my bushy mane was tamed.

Years later, when my daughter Shelley was in seventh grade, I walked into the bathroom and found her standing in front of the mirror, crying because she couldn't do anything with her hair. Yes—just like her mother, she has thick, curly red hair, and she was no more eager to accept my advice than I had been to listen to my mom's advice. Shelley got angry at my suggestions and comments, even when I told her, "Your hair is wonderful. You look fine." Eventually I realized, *She wants me to help her fix her hair so she can get mad at* me *rather than at her hair.* At that moment I identified with my mother, who had loved me through the turmoil of feeling young, awkward, and ugly.

My mother also believed that the world was to be seen and explored. (We were an Air Force family and lived in Japan and Turkey.) The summer before my senior year of high school, we moved from Turkey back to the United States, presenting the perfect opportunity to tour Europe. While my father remained in Turkey, my mom, my three sisters, and I arrived in Paris at the military hotel with small bags we could each carry, and five very large, heavy suitcases my mother confidently assumed we could store at the hotel.

As my mom gave these five bags to the American sergeant there, he replied, "No ma'am, we don't store luggage here." This was more than my mother could handle. She'd just finished weeks of packing and moving our entire household so we could return to the States. Now, she was by herself in Paris with four children and these huge bags. She simply burst into tears. What in the world would she do with five heavy pieces of luggage during an extended train trip through Europe with four children at her side?

The sight of the crying woman and her forlorn daughters and all that luggage changed the sergeant's mind. Still, my college-age sister and I realized that Mom needed help, so we offered to take the responsibility of managing the trip's details. She agreed, thus demonstrating her trust in us.

I will never forget that summer as I, at seventeen, took charge of the trip's finances. I exchanged money and paid bills, while my sister made the travel arrangements and shepherded us to hotels and sights. What a glorious adventure and a taste of independence this experience became!

After I graduated from college, I applied to be a flight attendant for Pan American and enjoyed flying the London and Frankfurt routes. I can trace my love for travel and adventure, for experiencing different cultural customs and foods, to my mother's enthusiasm as she prepared us for new places, and to the confidence she had in me at that moment of crisis.

I must confess that I moved through the early years of raising my own three girls oblivious to what had been required of my mother. But one day it occurred to me: My experience of motherhood had been hers as well—what she encountered, what she endured, and what she rejoiced in as she poured out her life as much as she knew how. To teach, to listen, to love, to challenge, and to be present both for the grand times and all the small moments comprised the most profound work I could ever do. I finally understood that my mother's own commitment and my father's nonverbal affirmation of her role in the home had given me a similar passion to be involved with my children's lives. I found a new joy in waiting patiently through the mundane activities for the amazing moments of wonder that make a mother's heart soar. What can replace this?

As I look at the image of my mother in the photograph, I am sure I know what she's thinking—the dreams, hopes, and fears she feels for herself and for her children—because I have those thoughts as well. Perhaps someday my daughters will be the ones looking at the photographs. In them, I will be the young mother, and they the curly-headed children. But they will know my mind and feelings as I know my mother's, and they will share my dreams and purposes for them with their own children. My mother's gift to me will cross many generations.

REFLECTION: *How can you help your children gain responsibility without waiting for a crisis?*

Sheryl Lemon Wunder is the mother of three grown daughters: Shelley Smith, Karen Tracy, and Laurie. Her family has expanded with the addition of two sons-in-law, Randall Smith and Steven Tracy. For thirteen years Sheryl and her husband, Jerry, were on staff with FamilyLife, a division of Campus Crusade for Christ. They currently live in East Asia. Sheryl graduated from the University of South Carolina and, with her husband, coauthored the book *Expressing Love in Your Marriage.* Her daughter's essay, "A Figure of Grace," is next.

Shelley Wunder Smith and her mother, Sheryl Lemon Wunder

Shelley Wunder Smith
Daughter of Sheryl Lemon Wunder

—◄—

A FIGURE OF GRACE

Whoso loves believes the impossible.

—Elizabeth Barrett Browning

know my mother through pictures.

When I was nine or ten, I liked to take down my mom's college yearbook from the rows of best-sellers on the shelves in our family room and turn to the photograph section in the middle. There, among the posed smiles of the debate club, the football team, the homecoming committee, and the class officers, I would find my mother on the full-length page she had all to herself. I could look at this picture for hours, at the young woman my mother used to be. In a teal evening gown, auburn hair curling just below her shoulders, she stood tall and straight, her body and face poised away from the camera, with the hint of a smile on her lips. In that picture, she seemed to me utterly mysterious—how did the woman who won a campus-wide beauty pageant become *my* mother?

The memory of that picture, and the power of that question, dazzled me, growing in my imagination when I became a teenager. My mother seemed perfect and invincible, and in my mind she was a goddess. Awkward and uneasy with my body, frequently driven to tears by my own unruly curls, and beset by mood swings no one—including me—could predict, I believed myself to be the ugly duckling who would never become a swan.

Like Saint George fighting a dragon, with great insight and understanding, my mother battled against my low self-image and the cruel comments of my peers when I couldn't seem to defend or sustain myself. She shared stories of her own adolescence—of

136

her reed-thin body with eyes too large for her face, and of eating lunch in a bathroom stall during junior high because she didn't want to face the other girls in the school cafeteria. She told me that she never understood how truly beautiful she was or believed herself worthy of love until she was midway through college. I listened to these stories and sensed that my mother's pain had been like mine, but still I wondered: Exactly how did that transformation take place? How did she get past junior high to the college picture?

Eventually I discovered other photographs in which I could see the same young woman, growing into the mother she was for me. A black-and-white shot with my father, her profile serene and luminous. Holding me as an infant on her lap (she was the same age I am now) in a short striped skirt that looked like something I could borrow from her closet. A close-up of the Wunder women—my mom, my sisters, and me—snapped in front of the twisted mesquite trees in our Arizona backyard when I was twelve. Her smile and wide eyes are unchanged from earlier years.

I am no longer that gangly, miserable-feeling young girl so bewildered by herself and by the world. I can look at pictures of my mother and me and see similarities in our eyes and in our smiles. Now that she also has become my friend, I realize how the world possesses a texture and shape peculiar to our perception. But in those same photographs, I can also see my mother's unconditional love and wisdom, which I yet hope to attain. A question, changed somewhat from my earlier years, continues to haunt me: What is this radiance that my mother carries with her, revealed in every smile, in how carefully she listens to those who need her, in how she raised her daughters and responds to her husband with quiet but unmistakable strength, and even in how she orders her house full of flowers, books, light, and invitation?

I think I may know the answer. It is the strength of spirit that comes from weathering storms by throwing herself on the mercy of the Lord and not giving in to bitterness or despair. It is the courage to speak with sincere kindness to and about someone else who is mostly prickles and stings. It is the respect and freedom she gives to others to be themselves, which made my friends adore her and eager to hang out at our house. It is the memory of her own fifteen-year-old traumas, and how she really just wanted someone to listen when she poured out her heart, and doing the same for her own girls as they lay weeping facedown on the bed. It is the faithfulness to move halfway across the world—just as Sarah followed Abraham—to East Asia because her husband has been called there, when she would rather sit on the back porch overlooking her joyous, magnificently blooming garden in the Deep South, drinking iced tea and talking to her sisters, waiting for grandchildren to play with. It is, simply enough, grace.

I still cannot fully comprehend the mysterious process that turned the unshaped girl I saw in photographs into this poised woman with an incandescent spirit. Perhaps I do not understand because I don't yet have children of my own, just as she did not fully know her own mother until she had daughters. Even now when I am with her, I watch her and wonder if my own children will do the same with me. I wonder if they will examine my pictures, timidly tracing my portrait with their fingertips, searching for their own swan shapes to be, and seeing, as the poet Mary Oliver puts it, "the light that can shine out of a life."

REFLECTION: *What do you want your children to remember when they look at your past pictures? What can you share from your past to connect with and relate to your children?*

Shelley Wunder Smith and her husband, Randall, have been married for four years and live in Chapel Hill, North Carolina. Shelley received a bachelor's degree in English from Auburn University and a master's degree in English from the University of North Carolina at Chapel Hill. She has two "charmingly naughty" cats named Emily and Taliafero. Shelley loves being at home, working in her flower garden, and reading. She is currently pursuing freelance editorial work and has a third-generation ice-cream addiction inherited from her mother's side of the family.

The Raineys at Ashley and Michael's wedding in 1997

MOTHERHOOD IS WORTH IT!

*J*ust before Christmas in 1965, thirty-four-year-old Marjorie sat stunned in the living room as her husband announced that he was leaving her for another woman. Three daughters and three sons, ranging in age from three months to fourteen years, sat with her in the living room and cried.

Marjorie walked shell-shocked through the next nine months, watching helplessly as her family slowly unraveled. But on September 23, 1966—her ex-husband's and her anniversary—Marjorie came to a profound conclusion. After returning from a meeting with her ex-husband, she realized that her family would fall apart unless she did something to stop it. There was no one else. It was up to her. And so on that September day, she gathered all six of her children around her and made a commitment to them and to herself. She declared with firm resolve, "With or without your dad, we *will* be a family."

Lofty goals are not achieved with ease and in comfort, and for Marjorie, her decision to keep her family together and to be a mother to all her children was one that demanded sacrifice. She decided to do whatever it took to provide for her family, but not at the expense of being a mom. She resolved that, no matter what, she would be at home when her kids returned from school and that she would be involved in their lives.

To accomplish her goal, she sewed draperies, mowed lawns, served as nanny to other children, and shoveled sidewalks when it snowed. She delivered newspapers with her kids. She watched every penny and not only put food on the table but also helped put most of her kids through college.

Often she would lie in bed at night and cry out to a God she hardly knew at the time. "Please help me raise my children. I can't do it on my own."

And God answered her prayers. Against all odds, her children are solid, responsible adults today, with families of their own. One of her sons, who was three years old when his dad left, is a dear friend of ours. We have had the privilege of meeting Marjorie, and I believe she is truly a saint. She is a mother whose influence on her children was profound as she modeled real family values for them, as she faithfully taught them right from wrong, and as she selflessly and sacrificially loved each one.

One of her daughters, Judy, wrote this about her mother:

> I would consider it a blessing to have as good a relationship with my children as I have with you. I look forward to staying up late with them talking, going to their ball games, being their biggest fan, as you were mine, and holding them close through good times and bad, letting them know that I'm there for them and that I love them. And I know I can do those things only because I have experienced a wonderful example of what a mother should be. I am proud and thankful that you are my mom. You've been a mother and a friend, and I love you, Mom, very much.

If Marjorie can be a successful mother, then I believe any of us can. Marjorie focused on what was truly the most important thing in life: her children. She ordered her life around what was essential for their well-being. She had her priorities in order, and, most important, she knew that she needed God's help to ultimately succeed.

Standing in the checkout line at the grocery store, I have often wondered about the women I see staring at me from glossy magazine covers, especially the ones who are mothers. They are usually supermodels or movie stars with a sweet innocent baby or toddler. Rarely is a mother of a teenager with an adoring teen featured on a magazine cover. *What kind of mothers are they?* I wonder.

The contrast I feel as I wait my turn to check out and pay is glaring. Those mothers look physically perfect. I usually feel far from perfect when I'm in the grocery store. And in those years when I was often at our local market with all six of my kids, my predominant emotion was feeling overwhelmed. I wanted out of the store, and I wanted my kids out of the store.

What a contrast! Marjorie and her brood, me and my half-dozen, or even my daughter Ashley and her first, compared with the images on the magazines. There is no comparison, if image is what matters. Is that what matters to a child? Do today's little boys and girls want Mommy to *look* nice or to *be* nice? Though I often felt tempted to fall into the comparison trap (and when I did, I came out of it with the "inferior" feeling reigning over my emotions), did my children notice? Did they care about external appearance?

Who is the better mother? It depends on what we value. It depends on what we believe. It depends on what we pursue.

In all the stories in this little book, there are several similarities. First, and most obvious, *none of these mothers was or is perfect.* Not one of these mothers did *all* of it right. Clearly, the perfect mother does not exist, and the perfect childhood has never been achieved.

Second, with what they had been handed in life, *all of these mothers did their best.* The alcoholic mother, the single mother, the grieving mother, the distant mother, the overwhelmed mother—all of them did the best they could. And the good news is that, with all the imperfections we can see, and with all the ones that were left between the lines, God is still in the business of redeeming people and of making good on His promise: "All things work together for good to those who love God, to those who are the called according to His purpose" (Rom. 8:28 NKJV).

In spite of their circumstances, in spite of their weaknesses, in spite of their personal obstacles, *these women chose to mother their children.* That alone is a significant gift each of us daughters has received. We all were given life.

All of these mothers chose to provide for their children, some simply, some lavishly. Each of these women taught their daughters by example or by verbal instruction, usually by both. And all sought to communicate love to their children, no matter how imperfectly. With our mothers, we all had opportunities to grow.

My good friend Karen Loritts, whose story "A Legacy of Tenacity" is in Part One, said this about her childhood: "I shouldn't be where I am today. I have been happily married for almost thirty years and have four wonderful children. But when I was a child living in the inner-city projects, raising my little brother while my mother worked to make ends meet, I experienced feelings of hopelessness. I knew my mother loved me, but I never felt it." Our immediate response is to feel sadness for Karen and her brother for the conditions they grew up in. And we should. No child should have to grow up in such difficult circumstances. But Karen quickly added, "Because I never felt loved by my mother, my heart was prepared to hear about God's love for me. And when I heard the good news, I dragged my little brother to church with me every chance I got."

Is God's grace sufficient for us as mothers or not? Absolutely yes. *If* we go to Him in dependence, willing for Him to work in us as well as in our circumstances and in our children.

The third common ingredient in all these stories is the similarity to their mothers found in the daughters who wrote their stories. As women we are vastly different in age, race, background, and ability. And yet we have all chosen to see our mothers through the lens of honor. To focus as a camera does on the most pleasing view, the most beautiful scene, the image we want to remember most.

Barbara Rosberg, another friend, whose story "Always There for Me" is in Part Three, wrote me a note a couple of months after she had submitted her story for this book. She had been given the opportunity to speak on "A Woman and Her Home" at a women's conference where her mother was in attendance. As she gave her talk, she paused and, without warning, asked her mother to come up on stage. She said, "I want to read something I have just written about my mother," and she turned to face her mom and read the story from this book. In her note about that moment, Barbara said:

> *Somehow in that hour I realized that my mom was the product of an alcoholic father and mother. In trying to cope, her mother had built a wall as thick as a fortress around her, but had unfortunately "walled out" on her kids (my mom) as well. So in that hour of obedience, I blessed my mom. I got to honor her in front of the world, and I pray that I ministered to places in my mom's soul that no one has ever gone—and guess what? I am free.*

Barbara saw her mother with the eyes of understanding and took the opportunity to bless her in spite of the imperfections she experienced in her mothering. To honor one's father and mother is a clear command of God, and it is also a great privilege. But that does not mean it is easy. While writing about their mothers, many of these women had to choose their focus, and in doing so had to give up or stop focusing on something else. That is the nature of honoring—it is moving from a place of discontent, anger, or resentment at what you were given to a place of gratitude, understanding, and peace, knowing that God is in control.

At the end of your life, what will give you peace about your years on this earth as a mother? What will your legacy be to your daughters? What lessons will they learn from you that they will be grateful you taught them? Will you feel contentment knowing that you looked the best you could, or that you *loved* the best you could? It's never too late to influence another, never too late to impart lessons and love to your children. You are their example of living well, aging gracefully, and dying with hope. Being a mother is a job that begins but never ends. The responsibilities change, but the title doesn't. May we as mothers diligently seek the Lord, that we might become all that He intended, and that our children might see more of Jesus in us.

Motherhood is really worth it!

ABOUT THE AUTHORS

BARBARA PETERSON RAINEY is the mother of six children—Ashley Escue, Benjamin, Samuel, Rebecca, Deborah, and Laura—and the grandmother of one, Samuel Alexander Escue. She and her husband, Dennis, live in Little Rock, Arkansas, where he is the director of FamilyLife, a division of Campus Crusade for Christ. Barbara is on the home stretch of raising her children, with only two teenagers left at home. When she is not busy with their lives, she enjoys seeing her new grandson, gardening, and reading. Barbara has coauthored several books with her husband, including *Parenting Today's Adolescent, Building Your Mate's Self-Esteem,* and *Moments Together for Couples.* Barbara graduated from the University of Arkansas.

ASHLEY RAINEY ESCUE is the mother of one son, Samuel Alexander. Two hobbies Ashley enjoys are collecting antiques and photography, but spending time with her husband and baby son is what she enjoys most. She graduated from the University of Mississippi with a degree in journalism and is a cohost on *Family Life This Week,* the weekend edition of the radio program *Family Life Today.* Ashley loves being a mom and can't wait to expand her family. She and her husband, Michael, live in Memphis, Tennessee, where he is attending medical school.

NOTES

1. Nancy Newton Verrier, *The Primal Wound* (Gateway Press, 1991).

2. Edith Schaeffer, *What Is a Family?* (Old Tappan, NJ: Fleming Revell Co., 1975), 44.

3. This prayer is often attributed to Reinhold Niebuhr (1892-1971), an American religious and social thinker. (Internet site: http://www.msu.edu/~vanhoose/quotes/005.html; accessed November 22, 1999.)

4. Patricia Daniels Cornwell, *A Time for Remembering: The Ruth Bell Graham Story* (San Francisco: Harper & Row, 1983), 145.

5. Helen B. Andelin, *Fascinating Womanhood* (New York: Bantam Books, 1992), 247.

6. John Bowlby, *Attachment,* Vol. 1 (New York: Basic Books, 1969), 204–205.

7. Peter Marshall and David Manuel, *The Light and the Glory* (Tarrytown, NY: Fleming H. Revell, 1977).